START EARLY, FINISH RICH

START EARLY, FINISH RICH

ANIL LAMBA

Bestselling author of ***Romancing the Balance Sheet***

HARPER BUSINESS

An Imprint of HarperCollins *Publishers*

First published in India by Harper Business 2025
An imprint of HarperCollins *Publishers*
HarperCollins *Publishers* India, Cyber City, Building 10-A,
Gurugram, Haryana-122002, India
www.harpercollins.co.in

2 4 6 8 10 9 7 5 3 1

P-ISBN: 978-93-6989-413-0
E-ISBN: 978-93-6989-848-0

Typeset in 13/15.6 Myriad Pro
by HarperCollins *Publishers* India Pvt. Ltd

Printed and bound at
Thomson Press (India) Ltd

HarperCollins Publishers, Macken House, 39/40 Mayor Street Upper,
Dublin 1, D01 C9W8, Ireland

Disclaimer

This book is dedicated to **Liam Lamba Heydecker**, our beloved first grandchild, as a small contribution towards making your generation financially smart and to empower you with the knowledge and confidence to make wise financial choices in building a secure future.

CONTENTS

WHY I WROTE THIS BOOK

Hi my young friends,

Much of my time is spent with far older people, who are about your parents' age, consulting and training them in matters related to the practice of good finance management in their businesses.

Almost all of them have expressed more than once in the course of my interactions that they wish this was taught to them when they were in school.

These people have invested large sums of money in their businesses, paid the price for the lack of financial literacy and intelligence and learnt the hard way the important role finance management plays in the success of any enterprise or endeavour.

This book is an attempt on my part to make you finance- and business-savvy early in life.

Children who are exposed to the subject while still in school would have an edge over others who do not understand it.

Also, the youngsters with an entrepreneurial mindset become founders of start-ups early in life. The chances of success of those who understand finance are far brighter than those who don't.

Many expensive mistakes which are made later on in life can be avoided.

It is also important that the habits of saving and investing are inculcated at a young age in order to enjoy the benefits of compounding.

This book will cover both the field of personal finance management as well as the knowledge and understanding required to make your business venture financially sound and healthy.

The intention behind penning this book is not to make you masters of the subject, but to give you a working knowledge of the terms in use, to introduce you to the various financial concepts and to give you a glimpse into the fascinating world of finance.

The objective is also to make you realize its importance, so that as you go ahead in life, you always remember that financial prudence lies behind the success of every venture and activity that you will take on.

I wish you much success, happiness and satisfaction in the careers and activities that you choose to pursue in the years to come.

Anil Lamba
July 2025

anil@lamconschool.com

PREAMBLE

There are two types of people in this world:

1. those who have money and don't know how to use it , and
2. those who can put it to good use but don't have enough.

The first category includes salary-earners, rental-income earners, people living off their savings, people whose source of earnings is interest on deposits, dividends on stock investments, etc.

The second category includes industrialists, business-persons, agriculturists et al.

The second group makes invaluable contribution to the nation's growth, pays the lion's share of taxes and helps generate employment in the country.

Obviously, the world goes around by the efforts of this category of people, whom all of you should try and emulate. You should strive to become job providers instead of job seekers.

In order to be successful as entrepreneurs, one of the most important skill-sets you must possess is that of money-management.

This book will introduce kids and young adults to the various aspects of finance management at an early age, so that when you are ready to take the leap, you can hit the ground running.

If you have a business idea, it will tell you how you can go about converting it to reality, the steps that you need to take.

It will arm you with knowledge about where to start, the legal constitution to choose and the pros and cons of each.

It will tell you how you can finance businesses—the various options available and the risks and benefits of each.

Having set up the business, you will learn how to manage it, the accounts that need to be maintained and how to understand the financial statements that will enable you to keep a finger on the pulse of your business.

Those interested in knowing how to invest, will learn how stock markets function and how you can go about investing in shares.

This book will also tell you about **how governments and nations raise and spend money** and how a country's finance management is different from that of an individual.

And many more things.

1

PART

A

IMPORTANT FINANCIAL AND INVESTMENT-RELATED CONCEPTS

IN THE BEGINNING

CHAPTER 01

Nobody can disagree that money plays a very important role in life.

But how did it all begin?

Hundreds of years back, when money was not yet invented, we had what is known as the barter system: If I make shirts and you grow wheat, I would offer you a shirt in exchange for a bag of wheat.

But the problem with this system was that, a few days later, I would need wheat again, but you may not want another shirt.

So the need for a common medium of exchange was felt.

Many different things were then experimented with as money, including cowrie shells and cattle.

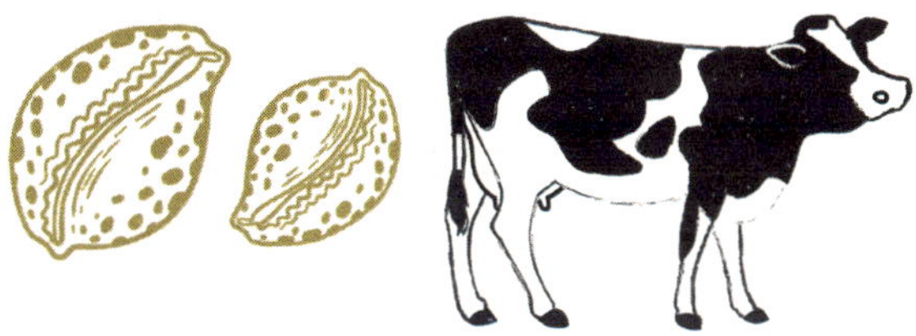

Subsequently, metal was used to make money. The earliest coins were made of copper.

However, copper being heavy, created its own set of problems when it had to be transported to make payments, particularly overseas.

Then the world discovered gold, which had many advantages—it was light in weight, had a lustre, was high in value, but its most important quality was it could withstand tremendous abuse—you could break it, smash it with a hammer, melt it on fire, without it losing any value.

While being light in weight was a big advantage over heavier metals like copper, it also brought with it a major disadvantage. One could be carrying a small fortune in a pouch in one's pocket

and become susceptible to being robbed and mugged. This fear spawned the mushrooming of 'pawnbrokers'. These were establishments with whom people could keep their gold for safe-keeping in exchange for a receipt. When wanting to make a purchase, one would present the receipt to the pawnbroker, collect the gold, and pay for the purchase.

Once it so happened that someone, wanting to buy something, didn't have the time to go to the pawnbroker's shop, and instead offered the receipt to the seller with a request that the seller directly collect the gold from the pawnbroker.

This is when it was realized that a piece of paper can be used as money.

Subsequently, it was decided that governments will keep aside gold and print money and any time a holder of paper money wished, the piece of paper could be exchanged for gold. This is how paper money came into being.

This system, where money is printed by keeping an equivalent value of gold aside, is called the '**gold standard**' and the currency is called '**hard currency**'.

If money is printed without the backing of a commodity like gold, it is called '**Fiat Money**' and the currency is called '**soft currency**.'

'The **best time** to **plant a tree** was 20 years ago. The second-best **time is now**.'

CHINESE PROVERB

THE AMAZING POWER OF COMPOUNDING

CHAPTER 02

What is compound interest?

If you make a deposit of 100 in a bank and earn interest at the rate of 10 per cent per annum, in year 1 you will earn 10.

If you withdraw the interest for your personal need keeping the principal intact, the following year you will again earn the same 10. If you withdraw the interest once again, the third year too you will earn 10.

This is simple interest.

But if you don't withdraw the interest amount in year 1 and leave it in the bank, the closing balance in your account at the end of year 1 will be 110.

The following year, you will earn interest at the rate of 10 per cent on 110, that is, you will earn 11.

If again the interest remains in your account, the balance would have increased to 121 and you will earn 12.1 as interest.

When you earn interest not only on the principal sum but also on the interest earned, **it is called compound interest**.

If you had kept your money in the bank for 10 years and were earning a simple interest of 10 per cent, at the end of the period you would have earned an interest of 100.

But if you were reinvesting the interest earned and earning compound interest, the interest earned by you would have been 160.

The difference in interest earned, though substantial, may still not appear to you to be very impressive.

But the benefit of compounding really comes to the fore over the long term.

Compounding can be done on a monthly, quarterly, half yearly or annual basis.

If the interest is calculated on an annual basis and added to the bank balance, it is called annual compounding.

In case of monthly compounding, each month the interest for the month is added to the account and the following month you earn interest on the principal plus the monthly interest.

Let us see the impact of compounding over an extended period of time.

Consider the following example:

EARNINGS			
Amount Invested = 10,000	Simple Interest	Yearly Compounding	Monthly Compounding
Year 1	1,000	1,000	1,047
Year 10	10,000	16,000	17,000
Year 25	25,000	98,300	1,10,500
Year 40	40,000	4,42,600	5,27,000
Year 50	50,000	11,63,900	14,43,700
Year 60	60,000	30,34,800	39,25,200

Take a thin sheet of paper, 0.001 cm in thickness.
Fold it in half, the thickness will be 0.002 cm.
Do it again: 0.004 cm. And again: 0.008. And again: 0.016 cm.

If you do it 10 times: 10 folds (that is, 2 raised to the power of 10) = 1.024 cm, which is a little bit over 1 cm.

If we fold it 17 times, we will get a thickness of 131 cm (just over 4 ft).

If we fold it 25 times, we will get 33,554 cm (just over 1,100 ft: almost as tall as the Empire State Building).

Pause and reflect for a moment: folding a paper in half—even a paper as fine as 0.001 cm—25 times would give us a paper almost a quarter of a mile high.

This kind of growth is called exponential growth.

30 times: the thickness reaches 6.67 miles
(about the average height that planes fly)
40 times: the thickness is 6,832 miles (nearly 7,000 miles)
48 times: 1,749,004 miles
If the distance from the earth and the moon is less than 2,50,000 miles, then starting with a piece of thin paper and folding it 45 times, we get to the moon.
And if we double it one more time, we get back to earth.
If the paper was thicker, it would require lesser number of folds to reach the moon.

The lesser the number of folds, the faster you reach the moon.

Here, thickness of the paper represents the initial investment of capital, and the number of folds is the period over which the amount remains invested.

It is often said that a person no less than Albert Einstein had called compound interest the most powerful force in the universe.

Whether he did say so or not, there is no doubt about the power of compound interest.

The story of the king and the farmer

There is a story of a king who played a game of chess with a simple farmer.

At the end of a closely fought game, the king lost.
Pleased with the farmer's effort, the king wanted to reward him and asked the farmer what he wanted.

The farmer said, 'Just give me one grain of wheat for the first

square of chess, and double it for each square thereafter' (which meant one grain for the first square, two for the second, four for the third, eight for the fourth and so on, for the 64 squares on the board).

The king readily agreed and the farmer's wish was granted.

When the total calculation was made, it worked out to 18,446,744,073,709,551,615 grains of wheat or over 700,000 million tonnes of wheat.

The farmer understood it and the king paid it.

No wonder the power of compounding has been called the eighth wonder of the world. One who understands it, earns it and the one who does not, pays it.

How can you benefit from the power of compounding?

You can make compounding work for you by:
1. Beginning the saving habit as early as possible and
2. Saving regularly.

If the power of compound interest is understood at a young age, the youth would have a great incentive for starting to save early.

Those who grasp the implications enjoy huge financial benefits. The sooner one learns about compound interest, the bigger the financial difference it can make.

The problem is that for the first few years, compounding does not appear very impressive. It's when compounding periods reach 15 to 30 years that the amount really starts to add up.
Compounding gives the maximum benefit when you let your savings or investment grow over a longer time horizon.
The earlier you start, the longer compounding can work for your money.

Take a look at this example illustrating the advantage of saving early:

Tony starts investing 1,000 per month at age 40 and earns an annual rate of interest of 8 per cent. At age 65, he would have accumulated 957,367 (on his total investment of 300,000 over a period of 25 years).

Tanya begins investing 1,000 per month at age 25, earning 8 per cent per annum and deposits for only 15 years till the age of 40. She would have a balance in her account at age 65 of 2,557,000 (on her total investment of 180,000).

Tony has invested for 25 years and Tanya has merely put aside the money for 15 years. And yet, at the age of retirement, the money available with Tanya is almost three times of what Tony has.

I would encourage all youngsters reading this book to start the habit of saving from tomorrow itself.

And I will urge parents of young children to invest some money in the children's account soon after the kids are born. If you do that, the child can have a saving horizon of about 60 years. You could deposit till the child starts earning, and thereafter the child starts depositing in an account that is already about 18 to 20 years old.

Such kids, by the time they reach retirement age, may just find that this account alone can sustain them for the rest of their lives.

‘

'The **greatest danger** for most of us is not that we **aim too high** and miss it, but that we **aim too low** and **reach it**.'

MICHELANGELO

THE RULE OF 72

CHAPTER 03

Are you aware of the rule of 72?

If you wish to understand how long it will take for your money to double, divide 72 by the rate of interest.

You can get a rough estimate of how many years it will take for the initial investment to duplicate itself.

If your money is growing at the rate of 6 per cent, then divide 72 by 6. In 12 years, the amount will double.

If the rate of interest is 8 per cent, 72/8 = 9.
The money will double in 9 years. And so on.

The rule of 72 is a simple way to estimate how long it will take for an investment to double in value, based on a fixed annual rate of interest. It's a handy tool for understanding the power of compound interest.

Keep in mind that the rule of 72 is just an estimate and may not be exact, but it's a helpful way to understand the concept of compounding interest.

Where can this rule be used?

The rule of 72 can be used in various practical applications, such as personal finance, investing and business planning.

For personal finance, it can help individuals estimate how long it will take for their savings to double at a certain interest rate, or how long it will take for their debt to double at a certain interest rate.

In investing, it can be used to estimate the potential growth of an investment over time.

For business planning, it can help in making projections for the growth of a company's assets or liabilities.

Overall, the rule of 72 is a useful tool for understanding the impact of compound interest in various financial scenarios.

What are its limitations?

There are some limitations to using the rule of 72 for investment planning.

The rule of 72 assumes a fixed annual rate of return, which may not always be the case in real-world investment scenarios.

It also does not take into account factors such as taxes, fees and market volatility, which can impact the actual growth of an investment.

Additionally, the rule of 72 is more accurate for interest rates between 6 per cent and 10 per cent, and becomes less accurate for interest rates outside of that range.

It is important to use the rule of 72 as a rough estimate and consider other factors when making investment decisions.

‘

'**Books** are the **quietest** and most constant of friends; they are the most **accessible** and **wisest of counsellors**, and the most **patient of teachers**.'

CHARLES W. ELIOT

CHAPTER 04

EFFECT OF INFLATION ON INVESTMENTS

What is inflation?

Inflation refers to a phenomenon of rising prices or falling purchasing powers.

Price, as you may well be aware, is a function of demand and supply.

When the demand for a product or commodity goes up, its price goes up.

When the supply of a product or commodity goes up, its price comes down.

(Inflation has been discussed in greater detail in Chapter 15)

Get off the treadmill

Effect of inflation is bad enough even when you are younger, since you need to make sure that your earnings grow faster than the rate of inflation. Else it will appear that you are making more money than before, whereas in real terms, the purchasing power of your income will actually be falling.

While you are still working, the impact of inflation is partially, or entirely, offset by a continuous increase in income or profit.

But inflation is a killer once you have stopped earning. If you have not invested wisely, it might well happen that the nest egg you have kept aside to live on post-retirement may not even suffice you for a few months.

The purchasing power of your savings dwindles as goods and services increase in price.

How much will you need to compensate for the impact of inflation?

Unfortunately, it is not possible to predict inflation with any precision.

So, if the expected rate of inflation is say 6 per cent (consistently year on year), as per the rule of 72, every 12 years (72/6 = 12) the prices would have doubled (or the purchasing power of money would become half in 12 years).

What costs 100 today, will cost 200 after 12 years, 400 after 24 years, and 800 after 36 years.

Which means if you are 24 years old today, and plan to retire at the age of 60 (36 years later), you will need to earn 8 times the amount you are earning today to maintain your existing standard of living.

Assuming a life expectancy of say 85 years, the amount required closer to age 85 would be 32 times your current earnings.

This calculation is based on maintaining your existing standards. But as your standard of living would be rising year after year, you would ideally expect the levels of comfort that you were enjoying at the time of retirement. So, the amount required would be even higher.

What can be done?

What steps can you take to ensure that your savings will take care of all your needs, despite the threat of inflation?

You are planning for the unknown since inflation is a moving target that really cannot be predicted.

In order to protect your interests and your family's well-being, you need to plan now to ensure the value of your investments stays ahead of inflation.

Which is why you must learn how to invest your money into avenues where the rate of earnings or appreciation is higher than the rate of inflation.

Inflation does not reduce the amount of money you have saved up. In fact, that amount may well be increasing due to interest earned. But it does reduce the buying power of that money.

With increasing costs of living, your ability to buy becomes lesser and lesser using the money available with you today.

If your money lies invested in a savings or even a fixed deposit account in a bank, the interest rate your money is earning is probably a lot less than the rate of inflation. Which means that the cost of goods and services is rising much faster than the interest you might be earning.

So what must you do?

Out of your concern for safety you may have invested in bonds and bank savings accounts. But these investments may not provide enough growth to outpace inflation.

You will have to move out of your comfort zone and invest in stocks and other instruments in order to add a level of growth to your portfolio that can keep you ahead of inflation.

Inflation is a fact of life. You, in your personal capacity, cannot do anything about it. You can only attempt to arrange your affairs to manage it.

‘

‘**Plan** for **the future** because that’s where you’re going to **spend the rest** of **your life**.’

MARK TWAIN

1738
1 2 3 4 – +
5 6 7 8 ×
9 0
17

PART B

PERSONAL FINANCE

CHAPTER 05

IMPORTANCE OF SAVINGS AND INVESTMENTS

It has been my consistent opinion that if there is going to be one stumbling block in this nation's phenomenal growth story, it will be the financial illiteracy of its people.

An individual's success in life, to a large extent, depends on the person's level of financial intelligence. And for a nation to achieve sustained growth and prosperity, it is essential that its people are financially literate.

It is an acknowledged fact that the single most important cause of business failures worldwide is financial mismanagement.

But this is equally true of individuals and families too. Otherwise, how does it happen that certain families with relatively lesser incomes appear to manage their expenses quite comfortably while others, having substantially higher earnings, are either perpetually running short of cash or seem always to be in debt?

It is not only in the interest of the economic health of a nation that financial literacy is important but also for the level of satisfaction and overall productivity of its population.

Those who cannot manage money are constantly running behind on monthly expenses and loan installments and find it difficult to make two ends meet.

They are also less satisfied with their life experience. And this results in a lower happiness quotient, which eventually reflects in lower productivity and inferior quality of whatever they do, make, or grow, and the vicious cycle becomes self-perpetuating.

The solution to many of mankind's problems lies in its ability to manage money.

And the earlier in life one acquires this skill, the greater will be the benefit.

If you improve finance management in nations, nations prosper. If you improve finance management in corporations, corporations flourish. If you improve finance management among individuals and families, individuals and families become financially secure, happier and more productive.

Effective personal finance management is necessary not only to enable individuals to lead comfortable lives, meet all financial responsibilities, educate their children and to eat and live well, but also to provide for the time when the income stops.

One should strive to see that post-retirement, the standard of one's living does not drop. In fact it should ideally enhance because one has more time available to be spend pursuing hobbies and travelling the world.

All this will be possible if we learn how to manage money.

The problem is that most of us either don't understand or do not have the time to do so.

We are completely engrossed in trying to generate more income (and there is nothing wrong with that).

But what has already been earned lies untended and unmanaged.

‘

'**Investing** should be more like **watching paint dry** or watching grass grow. If you want excitement, **take $800** and **go to Las Vegas**.'

PAUL SAMUELSON

INVESTING THROUGH MUTUAL FUNDS

CHAPTER 06

For passive investment of money, there are broadly two options.

1. Investing in stocks, which makes the buyer a part owner of the company invested in.

2. Investing in bonds, where the buyer lends money to the entity for a fixed period of time.

Bonds are also referred to as '**debt instruments**'.

Shareholders are rewarded by way of dividends, which is a distribution of profits, where as bond holders are paid an interest.

Both, stocks and bonds, are also collectively called '**securities**'.

How will you go about investing your money?

Let's say you are keen to invest your money in stocks and bonds, but don't know how to go about it.

This could be because you have no background in this field, or the subject of investment was never taught as part of your educational curicullum, or even maybe because you are busy in your professional or business activities and don't have the time to devote to investing.

And let's say you have hundreds of friends who are in a similar situation.

So, all of you decide to get together and pool your money into a common kitty, so that the amount to be invested is now a large sum. And then you hire a full-time professional to invest the money on your behalf.

Out of the earnings, the cost of running the fund can be met, including the salary of a full-time professional, and the balance can be divided amongst all the investors.

This is how a Mutual Fund functions.

What are Mutual Funds?

Mutual funds are a way for people to invest their money by pooling it together with other investors to buy a collection of stocks, bonds or other securities.

This allows people to invest in a diversified portfolio without

having to buy individual stocks or bonds themselves.

Mutual funds are managed by professional fund managers who make investment decisions on behalf of the investors.

They are a popular way to invest for the long term and can help people grow their money over time.

If a large number of individuals who do not possess the expertise, or are too busy to invest individually, pool in their money into a fund and the fund invests in stocks, bonds, and other assets on their behalf, it becomes a mutually beneficial exercise.

Since the amount becomes reasonably large, the fund can afford to hire professional money managers on a full-time basis who take investment decisions for the fund.

The fund charges the investors a small fee for managing the money.

The expenses incurred by the mutual fund are collectively called ***expense ratio*** which generally vary between 1.5-2.5 per cent of the average weekly net assets of the schemes.

Just as there are **shares** in companies, in a mutual fund one purchases **units**.

If a 100,000 persons purchase one unit each of 10, the amount available with the fund will now be one million.

This amount will now get invested in stocks and securities.

Let's assume, a little later, the market value of the one million worth of investments has become 1.5 million.

The market value is 1.5 million and the number of units are 100,000. So the value of each unit of 10 has now become 15. This is called the **NAV** or the **Net Asset Value** per unit.

If you divide the market value of the portfolio of assets that the fund has invested in (less its liabilities) by the number of units, you arrive at the per unit NAV or the Net Asset Value.

The NAV represents a fund's per unit market value.

This is the price at which investors buy fund units from a fund company or sell it back to the fund house.

New investors buying the units of this mutual fund will have to pay 15. And those who had originally purchased the units for 10, will be able to sell their units back to the Mutual Fund and get 15 in return.

NAV is calculated at the end of every market day, after taking into account the closing market prices of the portfolio's securities. For example, if a fund has assets of 60 million and liabilities of 10 million, it would have a **net asset value** of 50 million. If you divide the NAV of a fund by the number of outstanding units, you get the price per unit.

Types of Mutual Funds

In India, the Securities and Exchange Board of India has categorized mutual funds broadly into four categories:

1. Equity mutual funds:
These funds invest directly in stocks. Since equity markets are prone to fluctuations, these are high-risk, high-return schemes. These are useful for investors having a longer-term investment horizon of over five years.

2. Debt mutual funds:
These schemes invest in debt securities. Since debt is not subject to the vagaries of market fluctuations, these schemes are stable and substantially safe, but also provide mediocre returns. These funds would appeal to those looking to invest for short periods of less than five years.

3. Hybrid mutual funds:
These funds invest their money in a combination of equity and debt. The schemes of such funds provide returns which are higher than pure debt funds.

4. Solution-oriented mutual funds:
These mutual funds offer schemes for specific needs or purposes like children's education or for post-retirement. These schemes usually have a lock-in period of five years.

What is a Systematic Investment Plan?

A smart way of investing in mutual funds is through a Systematic Investment Plan or **SIP**.

SIPs allow you to invest a certain fixed amount at regular intervals of your choice—weekly, monthly, quarterly, etc.

It helps investors inculcate the habit of saving in a planned manner.

In case of a SIP the money gets deducted from your bank account on a standing instruction and gets invested into mutual fund schemes. The number of units that get allocated depends on the NAV on that day.

For each installment of investment, additional units of the scheme are purchased at the market rate and added to your account.

Over a period of time, since units are purchased at different rates, the investors get the benefit of **Cost Averaging**.

What is Cost Averaging?

Most people understand that one should buy a commodity when the price comes down and sell when the price goes up, but end up doing the opposite when it comes to investing in equity. In the absence of a Systematic Investment Plan, one would have to apply one's mind to time one's entry and exit from the market.

In volatile markets, this becomes difficult.

Cost averaging allows you to eliminate this uncertainty.

A SIP investor, while investing every month, would end up buying more units when markets go down and buying less units when the market goes up (since the amount to be invested remains fixed). It would help in achieving a lower average cost per unit.

‘

'**Don't leave anything for later**. Later the coffee gets cold. Later you lose interest. Later the day turns into night. Later people grow up. Later people grow old. Later life goes by. **Later you regret** not doing something when you had the chance.'

UNKNOWN

Chapter 07

Stock Market Investing

These days there is a huge interest among youngsters about stock markets. An increasing number of teenagers or those in their early twenties are beginning to invest in shares.

This is a very healthy trend and augurs well for the nation as a whole too.

How to Invest in Stocks

Let me start at the very beginning for the benefit of those of you who have never invested before.

There are two ways to invest in shares: through the **primary market** and the **secondary market**. The first involves purchasing shares straight from the company when it makes a public issue and the second when shares are purchased from existing holders.

When a company raises money for the first time by issuing shares (or bonds), it does so in the primary capital market through an **Initial Public Offering (IPO)**.

Subsequent public issues by companies already listed on the exchange are called **Follow-on Public Offers (FPOs)**.

If one does not purchase at the time of the Public Issue, or is not allotted shares because the issue is over-subscribed, the other option is to buy in the secondary market from the existing owners of these shares.

What is the difference between a stock market and other markets?

Which other markets do we know of?

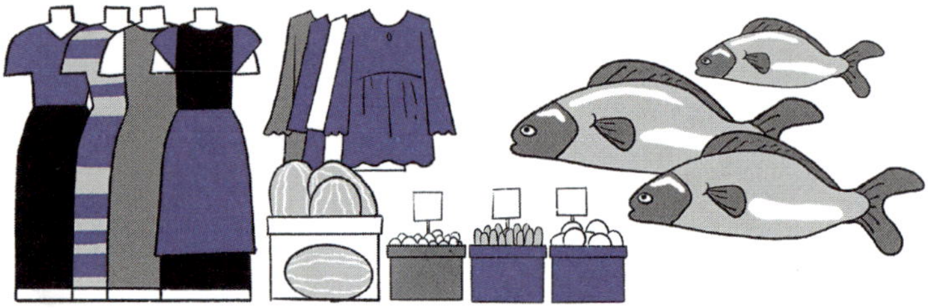

The textile market, the vegetable market, the fish market and so on.

What's the difference between these markets and the stock market?

The first difference is that in most other markets buyers and sellers meet face-to-face. In the stock exchange, this does not happen. Deals are done through brokers.

The second difference is that in other markets,
the seller carries the goods to be sold, the buyer goes with money in the pocket, and a physical exchange of goods for

money takes place. In the stock exchange, neither does the buyer pay money nor does the seller deliver the securities. Merely a deal is struck. The physical exchange of goods and money happens later.

How do you buy securities in the secondary market?

Let's say Tina has never purchased shares so far and wishes to begin investing.

(Let us assume that I am narrating a case that happened several years ago, when stock market operations were not yet fully automated and the settlement took almost a week.)

Early one morning, I receive a call from her saying she has kept aside a sum of 20,000 and wants to invest in shares, and if I could recommend a stock she should invest in. I suggest the name of Asian Industries.

Now how should she go about it?

The first thing she will have to do is to find out the price at which Asian is trading. She discovers Asian is trading at a price of 20.

She has to now find a broker with whom she can place an order to buy. (Of course, she can choose an online platform to do the trades, in which case the platform is the broker.)

Let's say, she identifies Broker A.

Broker A will want to know how many shares of Asian Industries she wishes to buy.

Tina has 20,000 to spare in her bank and the price of Asian shares is 20, so she places an order for 1,000 shares.

By evening, Broker A confirms the transaction.

So far only the deal has been confirmed. Neither has she paid for the shares nor received delivery.

The next morning, Tina is impatient to find out how Asian has performed in the stock market. She eagerly checks the price of Asian Industries and finds that it has increased to 22.

The following day the price has moved up to 25, and the next day she finds that Asian has touched 30.

Tina is excited. She thinks that since this is the first time she has ever invested, she better not get too greedy.

She picks up the phone, calls up Broker A and tells him she would like to sell her shares.

Broker A confirms shortly that her 1,000 shares have been sold at 30 each.

Tina makes a quick calculation of her return on investment. She had purchased the shares for 20,000 and sold them for 30,000. So she made a profit of 10,000 on an investment of 20,000 which works out to 50 per cent. But this profit was over a period of one week, and there are 52 weeks in a year. So 50 per cent multiplied by 52 weeks translates into an annualized return on investment of 2,600 per cent.

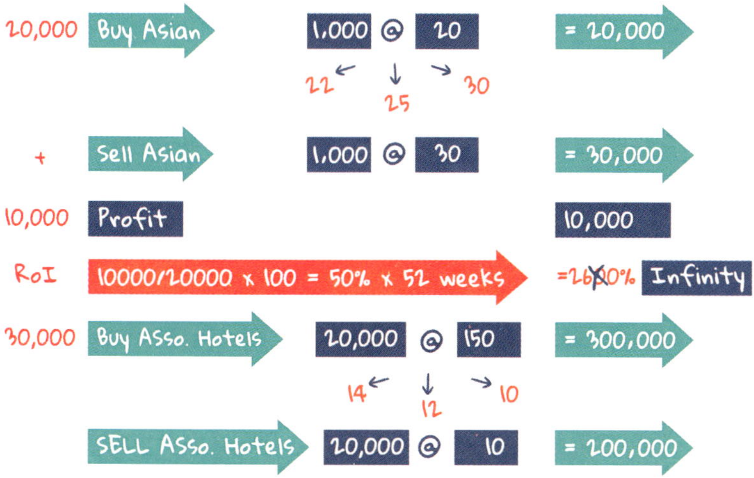

She regrets not having invested in stocks earlier, and begins to think there is no investment like stock investment.

Promptly, the next morning, I receive another call from her to ask what she should buy this time. Let's say, this time I recommend that she picks up stock in Associated Hotels.

The same process commences again. She checks the price and finds that Associated Hotels is trading at 15.

She calls Broker A.

He wants to know how many shares she would like him to buy for her.

The money now available with her is 30,000 (the original 20,000 plus the 10,000 profit made on the Asian deal) and the price of Associated Hotels is 15.

She can purchase 2,000 shares.

She is about to tell Broker A to purchase 2,000 shares for her when suddenly she stops in her tracks.

Why did she purchase just 1,000 shares of Asian the previous time? The answer was obvious: the price of Asian was 20 and the money available with her was 20,000.

But, she asks herself, did she pay for the shares?

Before she was asked to pay, she managed to sell the shares and make a profit of 10,000.

It strikes her that if she didn't have to pay, she could have purchased 10,000 shares instead of a mere 1,000, and made a profit of 100,000. Or, she could have purchased even more.

She also modifies the calculation of her return on investment which had worked out at 2,600 per cent. But this was on the assumption that she had made a profit of 10,000 on an investment of 20,000 over a week. But she now realizes that the profit of 10,000 was on zero investment and the return on investment actually worked out to infinity.

She snaps out of her stupor when she hears the broker asking her once again how many shares she would like him to buy.

'Buy 20,000 shares for me,' she says. With a bank balance of only 30,000, she has placed an order for shares worth 300,000.

The underlying logic applied by her is that, like the previous time, in the coming days the price of Associated Hotels would start rising. She would then sell the shares before the broker asks her to pay and pocket the difference.

Since she would not have to pay, she didn't have to confine her purchases to the funds available.

What she doesn't realize is that the previous time, my recommendation to buy Asian Industries' shares turned out to be correct by a stroke of luck.

The next day, when she checks the price of Associated Hotels, it has dropped to 14, the following day it is down to 12 and the next day to 10.

Soon the broker is going to ask her to pay up 300,000, which she does not have.

The second option would be to sell the 20,000 shares at 10 for 200,000 and pay the difference of 100,000.

Either way she stands to lose.

Investors and speculators

What I'm trying to tell you is that in the stock market you will encounter two types of players: **investors** and **speculators**.

Investors are people who purchase shares for which they have the money, pay for the shares and take delivery. They wait for an opportune time to sell, and when they sell, deliver the shares and collect the money.

Speculators, on the other hand, buy shares for which they may not possess the ability to pay, and before the due date for payment, sell the stock.

They pocket the difference if the price movement is favourable, or pay the difference if the price has moved adversely.

Investors will usually study the company, do some fundamental analysis and buy, provided the stock is available at or below its intrinsic value.

Speculators are akin to gamblers. They often buy stock not on the basis of its fundamentals, but on the likelihood of its price going up on account of market sentiment.

I would urge all of you reading this book to become investors, but avoid speculation unless you have understood all the risks associated with it and have the ability to bear the loss.

When speculators, expecting prices to rise, purchase shares beyond their means, it is called '**forward trading**' (also referred to as 'going long'). Inversely, when prices are expected to fall, speculators sell shares they do not have. This is called '**short selling**' (or 'going short').

Forward traders are also referred to as **'Bulls'** and short sellers as **'Bears'**.

In Indian equity markets, short selling is typically undertaken via the futures and options route and short selling in the cash market cannot be done for longer than an intra-day period, i.e., single trading session.

Investing in shares is a national duty

I have always maintained that investing in shares is not only in each individual's interest but is actually a national duty.

Why do I say so?

Let's first understand what a stock exchange is and what is its role.

The Stock Exchange is a market for shares and securities.

It is a place where buyers and sellers (through their representative brokers) meet and enter into deals for purchase and sale of stock and securities.

It is easier to appreciate the importance of a Stock Exchange if one visualizes what would happen if there were no such markets.

If a person holding shares in a certain company wanted to sell them, he would have to informally hunt for a buyer who would be interested in purchasing this particular stock from out of the millions of investors spread all over the country.

In the absence of a market, this by itself would be a gigantic task, almost like looking for a needle in a haystack.

However, having located a buyer he would have to negotiate, and if necessary bargain, to get a fair price.

Similar would be the case if one wanted to buy shares.

The Stock Exchange eliminates all these difficulties by providing a common place and having a mechanism for fixing the prices.

Why do I say that investing in shares is a national duty?

If an entrepreneur with a wonderful business idea invites you to invest in his project, and promises to return the money multiplied manyfold after, say, 25 years, chances are you will not agree to invest doesn't matter how attractive the proposal may be.

What will put you off is the long duration of 25 years before you can encash your investment.

On the other hand, if you are approached to invest in a business and you are told whenever you want your money, you can take it back, you will be far more inclined towards investing.

This is what the stock exchange does.

When you have money to spare, you can invest. And whenever you wish to have it back, you can call up a broker and ask the broker to sell your shares and get your money back. (You may get a little more or a little less than you invested, but the bulk of it can come back).

The stock exchange provides an exit route to the investor.

But this will not be the case if, due to lacklustre activity in the stock exchange, the broker is unable to find a buyer.

However when a large number of people invest in shares, the stock market is teeming with activity. Each time a person wishes to buy, he will be able to find a seller, each time a person wishes to sell, he will be able to find a buyer.

When buyers and sellers find it easier to locate each other, the investors have the confidence of getting the money back on short notice. This increases their willingness to invest.

When more people are willing to invest, more entrepreneurs are born, since they find it easier to raise money to finance their businesses and start-ups.

When more entrepreneurs come forward to start businesses, it leads to more employment in the country, more growth in the economy, increase in the nation's GDP and increase in tax collection.

And all this happens because you and I decided we should invest in shares.

How does the transaction take place?

When Tina approaches Broker A to purchase shares for her, it will not be possible for him to do so unless there is someone who wants to sell those shares.

Let's say, on the same day, Peter calls up Broker B to sell 1,000 shares of Asian Industries.

When Broker A and B meet (either physically, as in the days of floor-based trading, or virtually), a deal takes place.

Broker A will now send Tina a contract note which will essentially state that he has purchased 1,000 shares of Asian Industries on her behalf for which she owes him 20,000 and he owes her the delivery of 1,000 shares, both of which will happen in due course.

A little later, Tina will pay 20,000 to Broker A, who in turn will pay this money to the stock exchange. The stock exchange will pay 20,000 to Broker B, who will then give it to Peter.

The delivery of shares will take the reverse route. Peter will give 1,000 shares of Asian Industries to Broker B, which he will give to the stock exchange. The stock exchange will give these shares to Broker A, who will then pass them on to Tina.

In these days of dematerialized securities and electronic payments, all this happens automatically.

A person wishing to buy shares in the market places an order with a broker who routes the order through his system to the exchange. The order stays in the queue in the exchange's system and gets executed when the order logs on to the system within the buy limit that has been specified. The shares purchased are then sent to the buyer by the broker either in physical or demat format

What is the role of the stock exchange ?

The stock exchange acts as an authority that facilitates buying and selling of securities and ensures that each party honours its commitments.

In our example, Broker A had purchased 1,000 shares of Asian Industries for Tina from Broker B, who in turn was selling on behalf of Peter. However, the stock exchange does not recognize Tina and Peter. In the books of the stock exchange, Broker A has purchased and Broker B has sold the shares.

Broker A now owes the stock exchange 20,000 and the stock exchange owes Broker A delivery of 1,000 shares of Asian Industries.
Similarly, Broker B owes the stock exchange delivery of 1,000 shares of Asian Industries, and the stock exchange owes Broker B 20,000.

A little later, if Broker A sells shares worth 30,000 for another client, the stock exchange owes Broker A 10,000 (30,000 for shares sold less 20,000 for shares purchased by Broker A).

And let's say, Broker A sells 1,000 shares of Asian Industries for someone else. He had purchased 1,000 shares of Asian Industries for Tina, and now has sold the same quantity of shares of the same company for another client. The stock exchange moves out of the picture here. Broker A will collect shares from the client who has sold them and deliver the same to Tina.

The stock exchange is completely in the know of each transaction that has taken place and the money and shares due from and to every broker.

The net position of all the transactions that take place over a '**trading period**' are settled on the '**settlement date**'.

This is followed by the '**pay-in**', when brokers who owe money (because their purchases are greater than their sales) make the payments, and those who owe shares (because their sales have exceeded their purchases), deliver the shares.

And thereafter is the '**pay-out**', when the stock exchange pays money to brokers to whom it owes money, and delivers shares to those it owes shares.

Who decides share prices?

When Tina wanted to purchase Asian Industries' shares, she first looked up the stock market quotation and found that the scrip was trading at 20.

Who decided that the price should be 20? How was this price arrived at?

The prices appearing in the media are those at which the stock was actually traded in the stock exchange.

If you look up the stock quotations, against each company's name you will often discover one price appearing in brackets and up to four prices outside the brackets.

Now let's see what these indicate. If you are looking up this information today, the quotations will obviously be for yesterday's trading. The price in brackets in the diagram is the closing price of the day before yesterday.

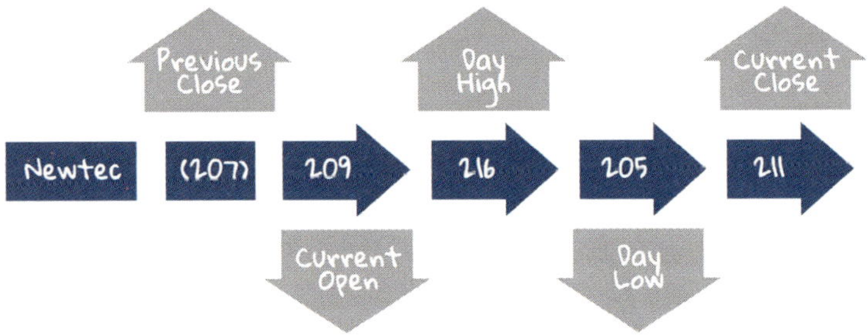

Let's say today is 15 December. The quotations will pertain to trading that took place on the 14th, and the price in brackets is the closing price at which the last transaction took place on the 13th (assuming the stock exchange was functioning on all the three days).

The first price after brackets as shown in the diagram is yesterday's opening price, or the price at which the first transaction took place on the 14th. The last price is the closing price of the 14th. And the other two reflect the highest and lowest prices of the day.

Hundreds of transactions involving millions of shares could have been transacted, but all at prices ranging between the highest and the lowest.

Who decides these prices?

Who decides that Asian Industries should trade at 20?

These prices are not fixed by any individual but are decided, as in the case of any market, by the forces of demand and supply.

Kris is at work when he receives a phone call from his wife asking him to pick up a kilogram of tomatoes on the way home.

The price at which tomatoes would be available would depend upon their production and supply. If there is scanty rainfall and a consequent shortage of tomatoes, the price will be high; and if there has been ample rainfall and tomatoes are available in abundance, the price will be lower.

Kris finds the market flooded with tomatoes and the price is 10 per kg. He picks up one kilo as instructed.

The following day, his wife asks for something else to be brought from the vegetable market.

When Kris reaches the market, he finds tomatoes are being sold at the price of 8 per kg. Even though he was not asked to bring tomatoes, he is tempted to do so. It's a cool evening, and tomato soup would be a good idea, he reasons.

The following day, Kris is at the market again looking for some lettuce leaves, and finds tomatoes being sold at 6 per kg. Another kg reaches the Kris household.

On the fourth day (he's been given a stiff warning by his wife that if he buys tomatoes again, she will not open the door for him), Kris, on a completely different errand at the market, trying not to even look at the tomato vendor while hurrying past, hears the vendor shout, 'Tomatoes for 1.50 per kg.' He can't help but give in.

Why does this happen?

When the supply of a commodity exceeds its demand, the price will tend to fall to a level where it will attract a buyer.

On the fourth day, if tomatoes were being sold at the rate of 5, or 4, or 3 per kg, Kris would not have purchased them. The price had to come down to a ridiculously low level of something like1.50 for him to be attracted.

The same thing happens in the stock market. If a stock is perceived to be overpriced and is being traded at say, 150, those holding the stock would be tempted to off-load and book a profit. But it may be difficult to find buyers who too may think that 150 is very high a price to pay for it.

Since there are not enough buyers, the holders of the stock (many of whom had purchased it at far lower prices anyway) may feel that even if they get 140, they would be willing to sell. If there are still no buyers, the offered price may be reduced further to 130 or 120.

It may then reach a level where there are investors who think that at 150 the stock is overpriced but at 120 it is attractive.

On the flip side, if a stock is trading at say, 100, and is considered a bargain at that price, there would be plenty of buyers. But the holders of the stock may think it is underpriced and will be reluctant to sell, expecting the price to move up further.

The buyers, keen to get in, offer 120.

If there are still no sellers, the offered price could increase to 140 or 150.

When it reaches, let's say 150, some holders would be tempted to book a profit, not knowing how much further it can go up and wanting to exit before the price starts falling again.

When the demand for a commodity exceeds its supply, the price will tend to rise to a level where it will eventually induce a holder of that commodity to part with it.

How do you go about investing in shares?

To be a successful investor, you need to understand two things:
1. What to buy and
2. When to buy (and, of course, when to sell).

1. What to buy

Selection of investment would involve the following:
(a) Choosing the industry which shows a potential for growth.
(b) To select the companies in whose shares or securities the investments are to be made.

2. When to buy and sell

The timing of buying and selling of securities is of crucial importance. Even if one can identify correctly the companies in whose shares the investments are to be made, one may lose money if the timing is inappropriate. The price at which the share is acquired for the portfolio depends entirely on the timing decision.

Let us first discuss how to decide 'what to buy'

How to identify high-potential industries and choose a fundamentally strong company?

Let me now tell you how to identify industries with a high growth potential and give you a shortcut to choosing a financially healthy company. Or rather, I will tell you which company not to choose, so that by the process of elimination, you are able to zero in on the company to invest in.

Identifying a fundamentally strong company in three steps:

Step 1

If you are interested in investing in stocks and wondering where to put your money, don't begin by choosing the company. First select the industry.

A reading of the business newspapers and publications, a glance at the government's annual budget or a quick search on the internet will give you an indication of the industries that have encouraging prospects in the coming years.

Study which sector the government is focusing its spending on (for example, infrastructure), which industries are being encouraged through endowments, grants, subsidies and incentives (energy, electric vehicles), which sectors are the flavour of the season (affordable housing) and on which sector the sun appears to be setting (coal, oil).

Once you have chosen the right industry, you would have eliminated a fair percentage of the possibilities of losing money.

Let's say you decide to invest in the pharmaceutical sector.

Step 2

The next question to be answered is, which company should you choose from within the pharmaceutical sector.

A company's growth potential can be roughly judged by studying its past performance. However, one should keep in mind that past performance and information is relevant only to the extent that it extends the future trends.

An illustrative list of factors that an analyst should take into consideration are:

1. **Size and ranking:** A rough idea of the size and ranking of the company within the economy in general and the industry in particular would help the investor in assessing the risk associated with the company.

2. **Growth record:** The growth in sales, net income, net capital employed and earnings per share of the company in the past few years should be examined.

3. **Financial analysis:** An analysis of its financial statements for the past few years with the help of certain fundamental ratios would help the investor in understanding the financial solvency and liquidity, the efficiency with which the funds are used, the profitability and the operating efficiency.

4. **Quality of management:** This intangible factor has a very important bearing on the value of the shares. Every investor knows that shares of certain business houses command a higher premium than those of similar companies managed by other business houses. This is because of the quality of management, the confidence that the investors have in a particular business house, the financial performance record of other companies in the same group, among other factors.

My suggestion would be that if you are a new investor, stick to the companies whose names come readily to mind when you think of the industry.

Which names spring to mind when you think of the pharmaceutical sector? These would be the companies that have been regularly written about, whose brands are well-known and can be considered to be market leaders.

There will be many occasions when some friend may call you with a recommendation to pick up a particular stock, a stock whose name you have never heard of. You may be told that it is now being traded at 15 and is expected to go up to as high as 100.

On being asked how this person is so sure that it will climb to 100, you may discover that your friend had received this 'tip' from another friend and being your wellwisher, had decided to pass it on to you.

On further prodding, you may find that the friend's friend had received the information from another friend, who had heard about it from yet another person and at the beginning of the chain, there probably would be someone with a vested interest trying to prop up the price of the scrip.

If enough people take interest, it may well happen that the price will go up for some time, during which period all the tipsters will stand vindicated. But at the first sign of a downturn in the market, this scrip may crash and even fade away from the stock market quotation pages, never to be heard of again.

At least for some time, till you become somewhat seasoned investors, I suggest that you stick to the known names.

Let's say you shortlist the following five scrips from the pharmaceutical industry:

1. Tabbot Labs
2. Prizer
3. Samson & Samson
4. Solvartis
5. Noche

(All the names of companies used in this book are fictitious, and if any name does happen to be the same as an existing company somewhere in the world, it is only coincidental.)

Step 3

Now you need to choose which among these five companies you should invest in.

For this, let me suggest certain criteria which the scrip must satisfy before you decide to invest in it.

A huge amount of information is available in financial publications and on investment-related websites.

Most of the information will be classified industry-wise.

From among the deluge of data you will be able to glean for each company in the sector, its sales, its gross profit, the net profit, the earnings per share, the price to earnings ratio and some more information.

Fundamental analysis

Company Name	Ye	Sales	GP	NP	EPS	PER
Tabbot Labs						
Prizer						
Samson & Samson						
Solvartis						
Noche						

Criterion 1: Sales

You can not only know the sales figure for the latest year-ending, but also the sales in the one or two quarters following (if the year had ended several months ago), and can go back a few years too.

I'd suggest you collect the data for a few years and plot a sales graph.

Do not buy the shares unless the sales graph is looking towards the sky.

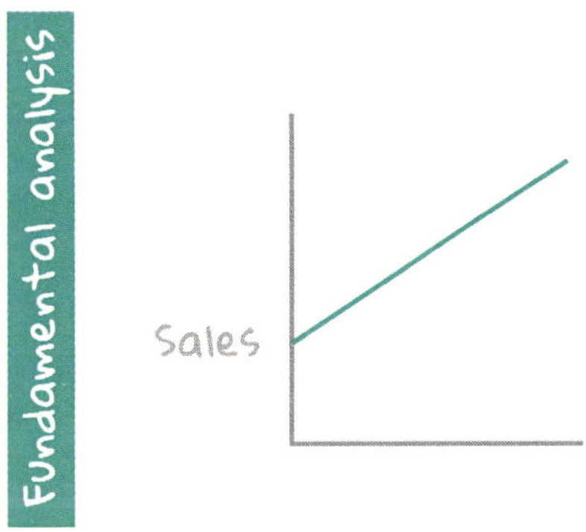

There are thousands of companies to choose from. Why would you want to go out of your way and pick up the shares of a company whose sales are either stagnating or have started to decline (unless you happen to be in possession of some inside information, in which case you must make a provision for getting prosecuted and going to jail too).

Criterion 2: Gross profit

Now look at the gross profit.

What should the gross profit graph look like?

Let's say, the sales in year 1 is 100 and the gross profit is 30. In year 2, if the sales figure doubles to 200, what should happen to the gross profit? Should the gross profit also double to 60? Or should it be less than 60? Or more than 60?

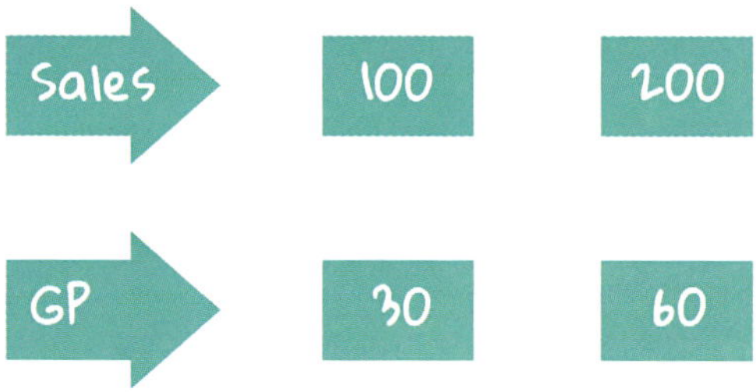

Gross profit is an accounting term and is arrived at by deducting direct cost from the sales revenue. When sales increase, the direct costs and consequently the gross profit increases in the same proportion. So if sales double, the gross profit will most likely also double.

If the gross profit more than doubles (however slightly), it is a great achievement, and if it less than doubles, there is reason to worry.

As Criterion 2, I would suggest that you do not buy the share unless the gross profit is growing at least at the same rate as the growth in sales.

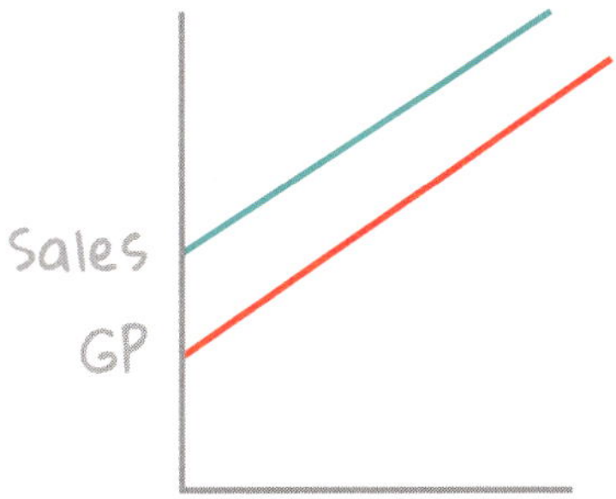

Criterion 3: Net profit

Now look at the net profit.
Net profit is arrived at by deducting the indirect costs from the gross profit. These costs are more or less fixed in nature.

If the sales has doubled, the gross profit must also double. But the fixed costs will either remain the same or will go up somewhat, and the net profit must more than double.

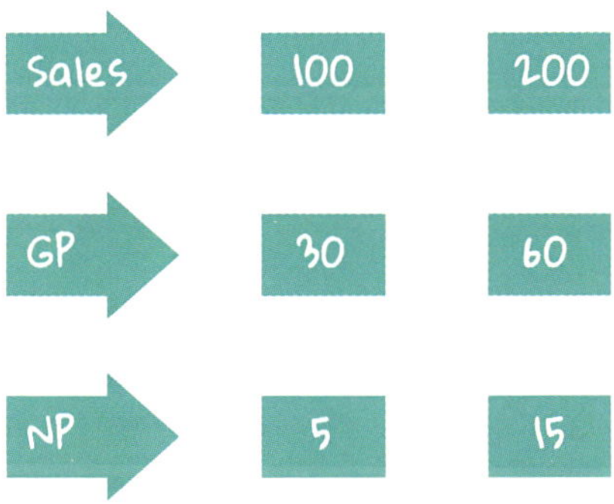

So as Criterion 3, ensure that the net profit graph is converging towards the sales graph.

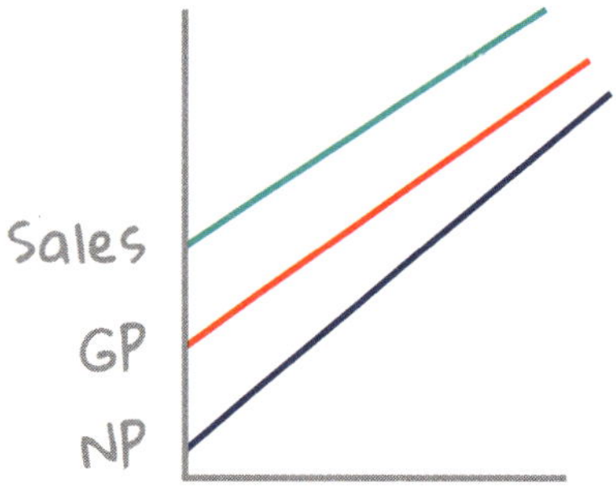

Criterion 4: Earnings per share

To calculate the earnings per share (EPS), first take a look at the Profit & Loss Account.

Let's say it reveals a Profit After Tax (PAT) of 600.

And the Balance Sheet shows a share capital of 1,000, which is made up of 100 shares, each carrying a face value of 10.

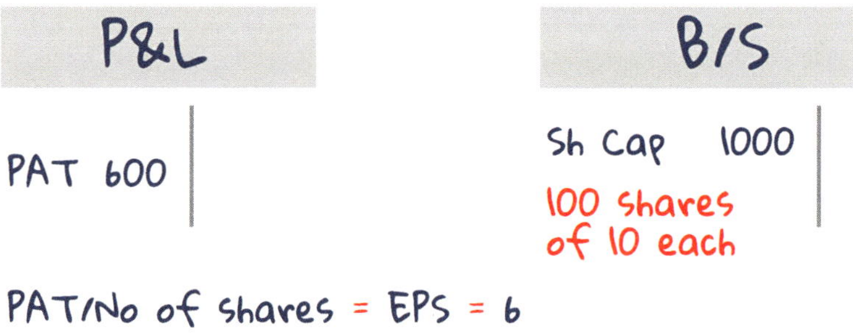

If you divide the PAT by the number of shares, you will get the EPS, (600/100), which in this case works out to 6.

Let's say the EPS of the five companies looks as shown in the chart below.

You can also find the composite average EPS for the industry given at the bottom of the chart, in this case of the pharmaceutical sector.

Company Name	Ye	Sales	GP	NP	EPS	PER
Tabbot Labs	xxx	xxx	xxx	xxx	5	
Prizer					15	
Samson & Samson					8	
Solvartis					22	
Noche					18	
Industry Composite Average					14	

As Criterion 4, I suggest that you make up your mind not to buy the share unless the EPS is above the industry average.

If the industry average is 14, it would mean there must be companies that have an EPS of 3 or 4 or 5 and also companies with an EPS of 20, 25 or even more. We are trying to identify a fundamentally strong company. I would not consider it to be one unless its EPS is greater than the industry average.

By the process of elimination, from the five shortlisted companies, Tabbot Labs and Samson & Samson are out since they do not fit the bill.

Criterion 5: Price to earnings ratio

Now look at the price to earnings ratio (PE ratio).

Market price divided by the EPS gives you the PE ratio.

PAT / No of shares = EPS = 6

Stock Market Price = 54

Mkt Price / EPS = PE Ratio = 9

If the market price of the shares of this company with an EPS of 6 is 54, the price (54) to earnings (6) ratio will work out to be 9 (54/6).

Let's say the PE ratios are as follows:

Company Name	Ye	Sales	GP	NP	EPS	PER
Tabbot Labs	xxx	xxx	xxx	xxx	5	6
Prizer					15	13
Samson & Samson					8	4
Solvartis					22	19
Noche					18	21
Industry Composite Average					14	16

I would now suggest, as Criterion 5, not to invest unless the PE ratio is below the industry average. By this criterion, Solvartis and Noche get eliminated too.

What are the first four criteria helping you with?

These are helping you choose a fundamentally strong company—a company whose sales are on the ascendant, the gross profit is also increasing at least at the same pace as the increase in sales, the net profit is growing at a pace faster than the growth in sales and the EPS is above the industry average.

Company Name	Ye	Sales	GP	NP	EPS	PER
Tabbot Labs	xxx	xxx	xxx	xxx	5	6
Prizer					15	13
Samson & Samson					8	4
Solvartis					22	19
Noche					18	21
Industry Composite Average					14	16

This is indeed a good company!

But do you necessarily want to invest in it?

If it is such a good company, chances are its stock is also trading at a high value.

Do you want to buy a wonderful share or do you want to make a profit? If the share is already trading at a very high value, the scope for making a profit gets reduced.

If you focus merely on selecting a good scrip, it may be too expensive. If you select a share which is available cheap, you may land up choosing a dud.

The first 4 criteria help you choose a strong, healthy, fundamentally sound company and the last criterion stops you from paying a very high price for it.

By the process of elimination we can now choose Prizer as it satisfies all the criteria.

Timing your entry and exit

Now that we have decided 'what to buy', an equally important decision to be taken is about 'when to buy' this stock.

The decision regarding timing of purchases is particularly difficult because of certain psychological factors.

It is quite obvious that if one wishes to make any gains, one should buy cheap and sell dear, that is, buy when the shares are selling at a low price and sell when they are at a high price.

Although this sounds easy, in practice it is very difficult.

An ordinary investor, on the contrary, normally buys when the prices have risen and sells when they have fallen.

When the prices are rising in the share market, everybody joins in the buying spree since the general environment is one of confidence.

Those who delay buying regret it, as every day prices touch a new high. The ordinary investor joins the buying rush when it is in full steam and, therefore, usually buys the shares at a high price.

When the downturn begins, an atmosphere of despondency pervades.

The ordinary investor panics and as every day the prices fall and reach a new low, he regrets not selling his shares the previous day. Ultimately, he sells the shares at a substantial loss, thanking his stars that he is out of the market.

This kind of an investment decision is essentially devoid of a sense of timing.

The reason why timing is important is because the most likely prospect is that the existing trend will continue. But the greatest profits come when trends change.

If a share is going up, it is most likely to continue going up. Yet, it is the investor who judges when it has reached the top and then sells, who will get the best price.

An investor has to view the problem of investment as one of buying and selling over a period during which the markets are sometimes in bull phases, that is, the prices are rising and sometimes in bear phases, that is, the prices are falling. At other times, the markets are stagnant, that is, there is no significant trend of rise or fall in prices. Investments are to be purchased when prices are low and sold when prices are high. This requires swimming against the general current in the market.

Hence, there must be an in-built system of timing the purchases or sale of investments, so that the psychological factors are ignored and purchases are made when the prices are entering the bull phase and sold when they are entering the bear phase.

If a graph is prepared of the share market prices and fluctuations therein, one would notice that the prices rise for a certain time, say for a year or two, and then fall and remain low for a year or two.

The best way to study the share market prices is to watch the share price index. The BSE Sensex and NSE NIFTY 50 are two important indices that investors regularly use in India.

Stock market investment strategy

There are many investment strategies to choose from. Let me share with you one, of many.

Let's imagine, after doing the industry research and the company analysis you purchased 1000 shares of a particular company at the rate of 100 each, making a total investment of one hundred thousand.

Before you even think of the profit that you can make, you must decide the loss you are willing to suffer and put a stop-loss limit.

You may decide that you do not want to lose more than10 per share. That is, in case the price of this share falls to 90, you will sell and get out. And you will not regret it if the price bounces back up.

But since you have done your study and timed your entry as discussed above, there is a greater chance that the price will move upward. Let's say, a little later, the price increases to 120.

What should you do now?

I want you to remember, two phrases that don't exist in the stock market are

1. Maximum profit and **2. Minimum loss.**

If you wait to maximize your profit, you may keep waiting forever. And if you wait to minimize the losses, the losses may keep mounting for each day of delay.

The time to make a profit, or a loss, is NOW.

You had purchased this scrip at 100 and the price has now moved up to 120. What should you do?

Sell a hundred shares at 120.

Why only 100 and not the entire lot?

That is because, if the price moves up further, you have more shares to sell. And in case it drops to below 100, you will lose less since the average cost of the remaining 900 shares is now lower than 100.
(Remember this is merely one of many strategies).

A little later, the price increases to 140. Sell another 100.

The price goes up to 160. Sell another 100.

The price now falls to 150. What should you do?

Buy back what you sold at 160 (provided the original logic applied at the time of buying the initial lot still holds).

Why should you buy it back?

You have sold the stock at 160 and purchased it back at 150. The shares are back with you and you have pocketed a profit of 1,000. What more can you ask for?

At every rise, you must sell; at every fall, buy back. Unless the price falls to 90, at which point you must sell the entire lot and get out; remember?

In fact, the stop loss must also be revised once you see the price has gone up first to 120 and then to 140. Why should you now be willing to lose anything at all? Maybe you should decide that you will sell the entire lot and exit if the price falls to 110. Above 110, at very rise you must sell and at every fall buy back.

Keep profits open-ended and put a stop-loss.

People often tend to do the reverse. They put a limit on the profit and keep their losses open-ended.

If the scrip that they have invested in appreciates a certain percentage points, they sell the entire lot, satisfied with the profit made. And if the price continues rising thereafter, they have no shares left to sell.

However, if the price falls below what they have paid for it, they keep hoping and praying that it will bounce back.

If you follow this as a rule, it will serve you well.

Word of caution: Don't let your portfolio become too unwieldy. There are some who don't invest in stocks at all. Others go overboard, having 100 to 150 scrips in the portfolio.

Nobody can be right every time. If you have such a large portfolio, at the best of times, half the scrips that you hold may be looking up and the other half down.

In my opinion, the number of scrips in the portfolio should be in single digit. This way relatively large sums of money can be invested in each and the amount of investment will justify spending more time on researching the stock well and also monitoring its price movements.

‘

'Either **write** something **worth reading** or **do** something **worth writing**.'

BENJAMIN FRANKLIN

IMPORTANCE OF INSURANCE

CHAPTER 08

Every individual and family must have adequate coverage of life insurance and medical (or health) insurance.

Insurance is important because it provides financial protection in case of unexpected events or emergencies.

It helps families manage risk and avoid financial hardship in difficult situations.

Life insurance can provide financial support for the family in the event of the death of the income earner and provides peace of mind and security during a difficult time.

Health insurance can help cover medical expenses if anyone gets sick or injured, while auto insurance provides financial protection in case of a car or a bike accident.

Let us talk about two types of insurance here—Life Insurance and Medical or Health Insurance.

A. Life Insurance

What is the rationale behind having a life insurance policy?

It is that if something happens to the breadwinner of the family, the person should not be missed at least so far as the financial contributions of the person to meet the family's expenditure are concerned.

An estimate should be made of the kind of income stream the family must continue to receive even if the income provider is no more.

For argument's sake, let's say that amount is 10,000 per month.

One must now work out the amount that should be left behind, in case one day the person is no more, to enable the family to continue to receive that income stream.

Let's say that sum is 1,000,000.

Who needs insurance more?

Who is more in need of insurance—a relatively richer person or the one who is poorer?

It is the latter.

If one has already accumulated assets of that value, one does not need insurance.

But if one does not own property of one million, it is possible to have an insurance policy for that amount by paying a fraction of that sum as a premium.

As one accumulates assets in other forms, the need for insurance progressively reduces.

The poorer a person is, the greater the need for insurance.

Paradoxically, it is the rich that usually are also insured, and the poor most often are not.

It is so important to be correctly insured. Most people are either under-insured or wrongly insured.

Which policy should be taken?

There are only three policies worth talking about when it comes to life insurance:

- **Whole life policy**

- **Endowment policy**

- **Term policy**

A **whole life policy** is one where the sum assured is never received by the person insured. When the person is no more, the insurance money goes to the beneficiary.

In the case of most whole life insurance plans, the amount and duration of premium payments are the same for as long as the insured is alive. But some whole life policies allow the premiums to be paid in a single installment, or for shorter periods or until age 65.

An **endowment policy** is a life insurance policy where a lump sum is paid on maturity of the policy or on death. Typical maturities are at 10, 15, or 20 years, up to a certain age limit.

A **term life insurance policy** provides pure insurance coverage at the lowest cost. There is no maturity amount to be paid in case the insured person survives the term of the policy.
It is similar to vehicle insurance where, in case the vehicle meets with an accident, one can claim the amount of damages from the insurance company, and in case no accident takes place, the premium is written off.

Since, in the case of both the endowment and whole life insurance plans, the premium paid along with a certain amount of interest and bonus is returned back to either the policyholder or the beneficiaries, these are considered to be savings plans that build cash value.

Endowments have a shorter coverage period and mature sooner, usually in 10 to 20 years.

Whole life policies are designed to last for the entire life of the insured, so these policies mature when the insured policyholder reaches the age of 95 or 100.

The term plan, on the other hand, is a pure expense since nothing is returned back if the insured person survives the term.

Endowment plans are the most expensive, having higher monthly premiums—the shorter the endowment term, the higher the premiums. Whole life policies have relatively lower premiums. Term policies work out the cheapest.

Whole life and endowment premiums are higher than term life insurance premiums since only a part of the premium goes towards insurance, and the balance is invested for future returns to be paid upon maturity.

This makes term policies the most attractive since one can take policies with substantially high coverage at affordable prices.

Never combine insurance and investment

Most people take insurance for the wrong reasons, such as to reduce their income tax liability (since premiums enjoy a deduction from taxable income), as an investment, or a combination of the two.

Life insurance has an important role to play in personal finance management. It is to protect one's family from financial difficulty.

Often a person takes a loan to purchase property—for example, an apartment in a building that is still under construction.

If, before the property has been acquired, the person happens to die, the family is neither in a position to pay the balance amount due toward the property nor to pay back the debt.

In such situations, if the person was insured, the money received from the insurance company can save the day.

But when insurance is perceived as an investment, one gets tempted to take the wrong type of policy.

There is a plan called the 'money back,' where a certain portion of the sum assured is paid back to the policyholder every five years.

It is one of the most popular plans sold by insurance companies.

The insurance agent makes it sound so attractive that most people opt for it. It is one of the worst policies to take.

Life insurance policies are taken for the benefit of the beneficiaries and not the person insured. The moment you plan to get the money back in your own lifetime, you have defeated the objective of taking life insurance.

Besides, I don't know of a worse investment than life insurance. What makes life insurance attractive is the package—the insurance coverage plus a mediocre investment.

However, if you keep the two separate—have pure insurance and a pure investment—you will get the best of both, an appropriate insurance coverage as well as an excellent investment, and may still have money to spare.

Instead of buying a money-back plan for a certain coverage, if you choose a term plan of the same value (or even a whole life policy of the same sum assured), you would have an equally good insurance at a far cheaper premium.

If you invest the leftover money anywhere else, you will probably earn more on that sum than you would have on the entire amount paid as a premium for a money-back plan.

Alternatively, if you have earmarked a certain amount that you would like to pay as a premium per annum, the sum assured that you will get if you opt for a whole life or a term plan would be substantially higher than what you will get from a money-back policy.

But the insurance agents will typically push for plans like money-back, not because these are better policies but because they get higher commissions by selling them.

You need to have the understanding to choose the most appropriate insurance policy to suit your requirement.

B. Medical Insurance

In addition to having an adequate life insurance policy, which is to take care of the family's financial needs after one's passing away, it is equally important to have the right health insurance.

This is to ensure that all the medical expenses of oneself and the family can be taken care of during one's lifetime.

Medical problems can take place without any prior intimation or warning and can potentially drain away one's entire life's savings and still fall short.

A small amount of money paid towards medical premium can help avoid financial trauma at the time of a medical emergency. A very important aspect of personal finance planning, therefore, is to arrange for suitable health insurance.

To secure the well-being of your family members and protect your savings while getting their medical treatments done from quality hospitals, choosing an appropriate family health cover plan is a wise decision.

This sort of comprehensive plan offers complete protection for each member of the family and can help lead a happier and healthier life ahead, free from all tensions.

As medical care advances and treatments improve, healthcare costs also increase. One is more likely to get routine and preventive care if one has health insurance. People with health insurance are more likely to have a regular doctor and to get care when they need it.

Today it is heartening to note that more and more people are opting for health insurance, even though we still have a long way to go.

Large segments of our population are not so covered, particularly among the poorer segments. And even if government schemes may exist, their awareness does not.

It is important to educate the masses about the need for medical insurance and the existence of free and/or affordable policies which are within the means of the poorest members of the community too.

For those who can afford to buy health insurance, the first step towards such a purchase is to understand and estimate your requirements. What is an adequate health cover plan is one of the most vital questions that need to be answered. You may need a plan for yourself as an individual, or you might be looking for a complete family health coverage plan. In either case, you will need to know the cost, terms & conditions, and services offered.

The easiest way to go about it would be to request a free quote on the website of the insurance company of your choice. All the major players in the insurance sector have their presence on this platform, providing complete, trustworthy, and valuable suggestions through online insurance.

What is the best time to buy a health insurance policy?

It is obvious that you should not wait until you or a family member becomes seriously ill to try to purchase health insurance. The right time to buy a health insurance policy is NOW.

Medical costs will only escalate in the future owing to the overall inflation and the rise in the cost of living, besides other factors. The sooner the realization of this truth sets in, the better it is.

It is best to buy a health insurance policy at a young age to avail of the many benefits.

Why should one get health insurance at a young age?

There are many reasons why opting for a health insurance policy at a young age is advisable. Most of these advantages serve to reduce the upfront and effective cost of the policy.

The premium charged on medical policies depends on the insured person's age at the time of taking the policy. If one opts for a policy at a young age, one can avail of a lower premium.

Many health plans offer wide coverage, the costs of which only increase as one grows older and owing to more medical complications. Taking a health insurance policy at a young age ensures that you have greater coverage.

Buying a health insurance policy in your late 40s will only increase your financial burden with reduced benefits. Many health insurance providers exclude many pre-existing conditions from getting covered, which defeats the purpose of opting for a health insurance policy.

Besides, health insurance premiums enjoy a tax rebate. Buying a health insurance policy at a young age allows one to enjoy tax benefits for a longer period, which also effectively reduces the out-of-pocket cost of the premium.

Most insurance companies offer a 'no claim bonus' in the absence of any claims in the preceding year of a policy term. If you buy a health insurance policy at a young age, you can avail of a cumulative bonus as you will most likely renew your policy every year. As a result, the bonus accumulated increases your coverage amount which will prove to be an advantage at later stages of life when you are old and grey. No-claim bonuses may range from 5 per cent to 100 per cent of the sum insured in most cases.

Most health insurance policies prescribe a waiting period of one to three months during which claims cannot be made even if

there is a medical emergency. Buying a health insurance policy at a young age when one is in robust health is advantageous as, barring a misfortune, the waiting period can be passed without any concern.

It also makes for good financial planning since buying a health insurance policy at a young age not only gives greater coverage but also helps in planning one's finances in a better way. When one has adequate medical cover to take care of any health emergencies, one can focus better on making other long-term investments.

Things to take care of while buying health insurance

Ensure to purchase a comprehensive mediclaim policy which provides sufficient coverage against future medical expenses. The medical policy should not only cover hospitalization but also pre- and post-hospitalization expenses.

Besides this, the plan chosen should offer coverage for OPD check-ups, dental treatment as well as maternity and critical illness coverage. To provide for serious illnesses like cancer or heart attack, the feature of lifelong renewal can be helpful.

'It's not **your salary** that makes you rich, it's your **spending habits**.'

CHARLES A. JAFFE

PART C

BUSINESS FINANCE

THE JOURNEY BEGINS

If I was right now in a room sitting face-to-face with you and asked you a question, 'How many of you, a few years down the line, would like to become entrepreneurs, would like to be founders of a start-up?'

Chances are many hands would go up.

Your success, when you do become founders, will to a large extent depend on how financially intelligent you are.

How will you go about starting your business?

You will first need an idea, decide what it is that you would like to do, what product you would like to make or sell, which problem of the world you would like to solve.

The next thing you will have to decide is the legal structure you will adopt for your business—are you going to run it as a proprietary concern, a partnership firm, a limited liability company or some other form of entity. *(The details about the pros and cons of each of these I will discuss in the next chapter.)*

Then, of course, you will need to figure out the amount of money you will need and where it will come from. *(This has been discussed in chapter 10).*

Then you will have to open a bank account *(the role of the bank is discussed in chapter 11)* and once the business is set up, you will have to keep track of the transactions that have taken place, (called accounting) and keep tabs in which direction the business is headed—which can be done by preparing financial statements like the Profit and Loss Statement and the Balance Sheet and reading and analysing these statements. *(Discussed in chapter 12.)*

Once you start making profit and earning money, you will also have to pay income tax. *(Discussed in chapter 13.)*

When the business starts to grow, every now and then, further need for money will crop up. Money will be required for day-to-day operations as well as to finance expansion and for scaling up the business.

And then, when you have acquired sufficient experience and are ready for the big leap, large sums of money will need to be raised. *(Discussed in chapter 14.)*

'Today **a reader**,
tomorrow **a leader**.'

MARGARET FULLER

CHAPTER 09

LEGAL STRUCTURES FOR RUNNING A BUSINESS

The legal structure that you select will depend upon a few factors like the cost involved for setting it up, the tax and other benefits associated with it and the legal requirements. Choosing the right one can greatly impact the success and growth of a business.

Types of business structures in India

You can run your business, amongst other options, as
- a Sole Proprietor,
- a Partnership Firm/a Limited Liability Partnership
- or a Company—which could either be a Private Limited or a Public Limited or a One-Person Company.

Before I proceed further, I want to explain two concepts to you—
1. The concept of limited liability and
2. The concept of an incorporated company

What does limited liability mean?

Let us first understand the meaning of liability.

When you start a business, there are risks involved.

Everything cannot be anticipated and planned. Certain unforeseen things can take place. Events over which you have no control (like the COVID pandemic) may occur and the business may incur losses and may not be in a position to meet the commitments made.

In such cases, its assets can be attached or sold in order to pay its liabilities.

But what if the value of the assets owned by the business is not sufficient to meet the liabilities?

In such cases, the business owners' personal assets (house, car, jewellery and other movable and immovable properties) can also be attached.

In other words, the liability of the business owner or promoter is unlimited, that is, it is not confined to the assets owned by the business alone but also extends to the personal assets.

However this will not be the case if the business is run as a Limited Liability Partnership (LLP) or a Company (Private Limited or Public Limited).

The word 'Limited' in Limited Liability Partnership, Private Limited Company, Public Limited Company, etc., indicates limited liability.

It means that only the business assets can be attached to meet its liabilities and the personal assets of the owner cannot be used to pay off the business's liabilities.

This concept encourages entrepreneurship and allows people to take risks without fear of losing everything they own. It's like having a safety net for your personal finances while running a business.

Limited liability can make a business more attractive to potential investors because it limits their financial risk. With limited liability, investors can feel more comfortable putting their money into a business knowing that their personal assets are not at risk if the business fails. This can make it easier for businesses to attract investors and raise capital, as it provides a level of protection for those investing in the company.

What does 'incorporating a company' mean?

Incorporating a company refers to the legal process of forming a new business entity that is recognized as a separate legal entity from its owners. It is almost like giving birth to a child.

Just as a child is a separate entity from the parents, similarly once a private or a public limited company is formed, it becomes a legal entity distinct from the owners that formed it.

For example, Mr Dhirubhai Ambani started a company called Reliance Industries Ltd. Now Reliance becomes a separate entity from Dhirubhai.

You and I are natural persons. A company is a legal person. Natural persons can die, but companies have perpetual existence. Mr Dhirubhai Ambani is no more, but Reliance continues to live till date. This is not the case with sole proprietorships and partnership firms. Their identity is the same as the identity of the owners.

Which structure should you choose for your business?

I would suggest to choose one out of these four options:
1. Sole Proprietorship
2. A One-Person Company
3. A Limited Liability Partnership Firm
4. A Private Limited Company

If you are the single owner of your business, then the options open to you are

1. to run it as a Sole Proprietorship Concern or
2. to start a One-Person Company

If two or more owners are starting a business together, then the options to choose from are:

3. a Limited Liability Partnership—LLP or
4. a Private Limited Company.

Let us understand each of these.

1. Sole proprietorship:

A sole proprietorship is a non-registered business run solely by one individual proprietor with no distinction between the business and the owner. The owner of a sole proprietorship is entitled to all profits but is also responsible for the business's debts, losses and liabilities.

Advantages of sole proprietorships

Sole proprietorships are easy to establish and dismantle due to lack of government involvement, making them popular with small business owners.
Most small businesses start as sole proprietorships and end up transitioning to a limited liability entity or corporation as the company grows.

What are the disadvantages of a sole proprietorship?

Owners are liable for all debts and obligations and there is unlimited personal liability. Sole proprietorship attract higher tax rates compared to other models. Financing and business credit is harder to procure.

2. One Person Company (OPC):

This is a type of business entity that allows a single person to start and operate a company. This is a relatively new concept in India.

Advantages of OPC

The key benefit of OPC is that it provides limited liability to the sole owner, which means their personal assets are protected from business debts and obligations. This can encourage more individuals to start their own businesses without the fear of losing everything they own in case of failure.

Additionally, OPCs have less compliance requirements compared to other types of companies, making it easier for individuals to manage their business on their own.

Disadvantages of OPC

However, some disadvantages of OPC include restrictions on the number of employees and turnover, as well as the requirement for the owner to convert the OPC into a private limited company if the annual turnover exceeds a certain limit.

OPCs may also face challenges in raising funds and attracting investors due to the perception of higher risk associated with a single-owner business.

Overall, while OPCs offer benefits such as limited liability and simplified compliance, they also come with limitations and potential challenges in terms of growth and scalability.

3. A Limited Liability Partnership:

A Limited Liability Partnership is incorporated under the Limited Liability Partnership Act 2009.

Partners in a normal partnership firm have unlimited liabilities, but the liability of those in an LLP is limited. Their responsibility towards losses or debts is limited to investments made by them.

A limited liability partnership and its partners are considered separate legal entities.

An LLP can be started with no minimum amount of capital contribution (unlike that in case of a company). It is an easy process to start an LLP as compared to a private company, along with lesser legal requirements.

There need to be a minimum of two partners in this form of legal structure. There is no upper limit on the number of business owners.

The cost of registration is lesser as compared to a private limited company.

The legal compliance requirements are comparatively less than in case of Private Limited Companies.

4. A Private Limited Company:

Most start-ups and businesses in India with higher ambitions choose Private Limited Company as the business structure of choice.

A Private Limited Company is a separate legal entity.
An entity means something which has a legal existence; therefore, the company can sue and can also be sued under its name.

It is able to borrow more funds than LLPs as it has more options for taking on debt as compared to OPCs and LLPs.

Even banks and other financial institutions prefer private limited companies over partnership entities to give loans to.

Private limited companies can be sold or transferred, either partially or in full, to another individual or entity without any disruption to the current business.

It has perpetual existence. The company's existence remains unaffected by the death or resignation of any member.

'**Great things** are not done by impulse, but by a series of **small things** brought together. The trick is to focus on the **first small thing**. Starting small is still starting, and small beginnings often lead to **extraordinary endings**.'

VINCENT VAN GOGH

CHAPTER 10

WAYS TO FINANCE A BUSINESS

Broadly speaking, all fund raising is either by way of investing equity or taking debt.

Equity represents the promoters' own money or from others who are made partners or co-owners in exchange for the money invested and who get to share the profits.

Debt is when a company borrows money from a bank or other lender and agrees to pay it back with interest. This is like taking out a loan.

Debt has to be paid back, while equity is a more permanent investment in the company. Both options have their advantages and disadvantages, and businesses have to decide which one is best for them.

A business might choose debt over equity if they want to maintain full control of their company and do not want to share the ownership with others.

Additionally, if the business has a steady and predictable cash flow, it may be more inclined to take on debt as it can confidently make regular payments.

On the other hand, a business might choose equity over debt if they are in a high-growth phase and need more flexibility with their finances. Equity investors also provide more than just money—they often bring valuable expertise and connections to the table.

How are start-ups typically funded?

There are several ways that a start-up can be funded. One common method is through personal savings or investments from friends and family.

This is also known as bootstrapping.

Bootstrapping

Bootstrapping refers to the practice of starting and growing a business using only personal finances or operating revenues. This means that the start-up does not seek external funding from investors, banks or other sources. Instead, the founders rely on their own savings, revenue generated by the business, or other creative means to fund the company's operations and growth. Bootstrapping requires careful financial management and often involves making sacrifices in the short term in order to achieve long-term success. It can be a challenging but rewarding way for entrepreneurs to build their businesses without taking on external debt or giving up ownership to investors.

Another option is to seek funding from angel investors or venture capitalists who are willing to provide capital in exchange for equity in the company.

Angel investors

Angel investors are individuals who provide financial backing to start-ups in exchange for ownership equity or convertible debt. Convertible debt is a type of loan that can be converted into shares at a later stage. It's like lending money to a company with the option to later exchange that debt for ownership in the company. They are typically wealthy individuals who invest their own money into early-stage companies with the goal of helping them grow and succeed. Angel investors often provide mentorship, advice and networking opportunities in addition to funding, and they play a crucial role in supporting the development of new businesses.

Start-ups can also apply for business loans from banks or other financial institutions.

Additionally, crowdfunding platforms like Kickstarter or Indiegogo can be used to raise funds from a large number of people.

Crowdfunding

Crowdfunding is a way for people to raise money for a project or cause by asking a large number of people to each contribute a small amount of money. It's like having a big group of friends all chip in a little bit of money to help someone achieve their goal. This could be for things like starting a new business, making a movie or helping someone in need. People can donate money online through crowdfunding platforms and in return, they might receive a small reward or special recognition for their support. It's a way for everyone to come together and make big things happen.

Finally, some start-ups may qualify for government grants or subsidies aimed at supporting small businesses.

Government grants or subsidies

Government grants or subsidies for start-ups are financial assistance provided by the government to help new businesses get off the ground. It's like the government giving a special gift to someone who wants to start a business.

This support can come in the form of money, resources or tax breaks to help entrepreneurs turn their ideas into reality. The government wants to encourage innovation and job creation, so they offer these grants and subsidies to help start-ups succeed. It's like a helping hand from the government to make it easier for new businesses to get started.

Some successful start-ups that used personal savings or investments from friends and family include **Apple** and **Google**. Both companies were initially funded by personal savings and investments from friends and family before they became the tech giants they are today.

For angel investors or venture capitalists, companies like **Uber** and **Airbnb** received funding from these sources in their early stages.

As for business loans, companies like **Warby Parker** and **Blue Apron** used this method to finance their operations.

Crowdfunding platforms have been utilized by start-ups such as **Oculus VR**, which raised funds on **Kickstarter** before being acquired by Facebook.

And finally, government grants or subsidies have been used by companies like **Tesla** and **SolarCity** to support their growth and development.

Stages of funding

The different stages of funding for a start-up typically include
pre-seed funding,
seed funding,
early-stage funding, and
later-stage funding.

Pre-seed funding is the initial capital raised to develop a business idea and create a prototype.

Typical sources of pre-seed funding for start-ups include personal savings, investments from friends and family, and grants or competitions aimed at supporting early-stage entrepreneurs. Some start-ups may also seek pre-seed funding from angel investors or accelerators.

Seed funding is the next stage, which is used to launch the product or service and begin marketing and sales efforts.

Seed money refers to the initial capital that is invested in a start-up to help it get off the ground. It is like planting a seed in the ground to create a new plant or tree. The seed money is used to cover the early expenses of the business, such as developing a product or service, conducting market research and setting up operations. This initial funding is crucial for start-ups to begin their journey and grow into successful businesses.

Common sources of seed money for start-ups include personal savings, investments from friends and family, angel investors, and crowdfunding platforms. Start-ups may also receive seed funding from incubators in exchange for equity in the company. Additionally, some start-ups may qualify for government grants or subsidies aimed at supporting small businesses.

Early-stage funding comes after the business has gained some traction and is used to further develop the product, expand the team, and scale operations.

It typically occurs after the idea has been validated but before the company has scaled significantly or reached profitability. This stage of funding is crucial for start-ups to develop their products, test their business models, hire initial teams and begin market traction.

Common sources of early-stage funding include bootstrapping, angel investors, crowdfunding and some accelerators and incubators.

Series A, B, C, etc. funding

Series A, B, C, etc funding refers to the different rounds of investment that a start-up receives as it grows and develops. Each round represents a new influx of capital from investors, which allows the start-up to expand its operations, develop new products or enter new markets.

The letter designation (A, B, C, etc.) indicates the order in which the rounds of funding occur, with Series A being the first major round of investment after the initial seed funding. As the start-up progresses and achieves new milestones, it may seek additional rounds of funding, such as Series B, C, and so on, to fuel its continued growth and success.

Typical sources of Series A, B, C, etc., funding for start-ups include venture capital firms, private equity investors and corporate investors. These investors provide larger amounts of capital in exchange for equity in the company, and they often have specific criteria and expectations for the start-ups they choose to invest in.

Additionally, some start-ups may also receive funding from existing investors who participate in subsequent rounds, as well as from strategic partners or industry-specific funds. Overall, the sources of funding for each round may vary depending on the start-up's industry, growth stage and specific funding needs.

'I often **quote myself**. It adds **spice** to my **conversation**.'

GEORGE BERNARD SHAW

CHAPTER 11

THE CRUCIAL ROLE OF BANKS

Banks play a crucial role in the economy by providing a safe place for people to keep their money and by lending money to individuals and businesses. Let's dive deeper into the functioning of a bank and its various roles.

The genesis of banks

Karl Marx, the father of communism, was of the opinion that the population can be divided into two main classes—

Haves (those who own means of production) and
Have nots (those who do not).

On similar lines, I have always felt there are two types of people in this world: I call them the **have-and-know-nots**—those who have money and don't know how to use it—and the **know-and-have-nots**—those who can put it to good use but don't have enough.

As I mentioned at the start of this book, the growth and prosperity of a nation is largely due to the efforts of the second category of people.

It therefore logically follows that, if one group is having funds that are lying idle and another group can put the funds to productive use, the money should be taken from the first category and given to the second category of people.

Earlier this was done in an unstructured fashion and the money was provided to entrepreneurs through private money lenders who were largely unregulated. Subsequently, the concept of a bank was created, whose primary role was to borrow money from those who have excess of it and lend it to those who can put it to good use.

One can well imagine what a tremendous marketing exercise this must have been, to convince people not to keep the money with themselves at home, probably in earthen pots, hidden somewhere beneath the ground or in containers of grains, and to instead give it to an entity called a bank.

The biggest hurdle must have been the trust-deficit— how can these people trust the bank to keep it safe for them and that it will return the money whenever they want it back?

But greed always wins. What most likely must have worked is when the depositors were told that at home the money earns nothing, but if it is kept in the bank, they will get some interest on it, say 10 per cent.

But the question was, how will the banks pay interest?

So the industrialists and entrepreneurs, to whom this money would be lent, were told, that 'you pay us 10 per cent so that we can pay the depositors the interest.'

Then came the question, if the bank charges 10 per cent from its borrowers and pays 10 per cent to its depositors, how will it run the bank?

A bank has expenses to meet. It needs to pay salaries, it has to pay rent, it has to spend on overheads. It also needs to buy equipment and furniture and many other things.

So, the borrowers were told they must pay 12 per cent, and the bank will pay 10 per cent to its depositors and use the extra 2 per cent to meet its own expenses.

Which is the reason there is a differential between the interest paid by the bank to its depositors and the interest charged by it from its customers.

But this also meant that the bank will have to lend every penny that it has borrowed.

The essential philosophy on which a bank works is that the depositors should not think their money has been lent out further, because then they will worry about the safety of their deposit in case the borrowers fail to return it. The depositors should feel that the money has been kept in a safe deposit locker in the bank, that whenever they want the money back, the bank will promptly return it.

So it is important that a bank doesn't lend all the money that it borrows from the depositors. A certain amount should always be retained, so that whenever any depositor comes to withdraw the money, the bank should be able to give it.

However, ultimately banking is a business, and it can happen there are times when a bank has excess funds lying with it (on which it is paying interest but not earning anything since it has not been lent), and it is refusing to lend it, out of a concern that some depositor may wish to withdraw, and in the process is losing opportunities to earn on it.

It is quite possible in such cases a bank may get tempted to lend these extra funds too and earn some more money.

But the entire credibility of a bank, and in fact the entire foundation of a bank, rests on the proposition that it doesn't matter how many times a banker is sitting on excess funds and no one comes to withdraw it, but it should not happen even once that a depositor comes to withdraw and the bank is unable to give it back.

In such situations there can be a 'run' on the bank, that is, in a state of panic, even those who don't need the money may come asking to withdraw their money out of fear that the bank is probably becoming insolvent.

If this happens, even banks which are otherwise fine and healthy can get into serious trouble.

So maintaining this discipline, of keeping aside a certain percentage of the deposits received, is of utmost importance in the banking industry, and to ensure compliance, it is essential that there is someone like a headmaster with a stick who is empowered to take disciplinary action if any bank violates the norms.

The role of the headmaster is played by the central bank in each country. In India, the central bank is called the **Reserve Bank of India**, or the RBI. In Great Britain, it is called the **Bank of England** and in the US of A, this role is played by the **Federal Reserve** (or the Fed).

The RBI in India lays down certain rules about how much of its deposits a bank is permitted to lend, and how much should be kept as cash reserves, and a certain percentage of its deposits a bank has to invest in securities.

These percentages and amounts, in banking parlance, are called the CRR (Cash Reserve Ratio) and the SLR (Statutory Liquidity Ratio).

To summarize:

A bank is a place where people can keep their money safe and also borrow money when they need it. It's like a big piggy bank for grown-ups! When you put your money in a bank, it's called a deposit, and the bank keeps it safe for you. In return, the bank pays you a little bit of extra money, called interest, for keeping your money there.

Banks also lend money to people who need it, like when someone wants to buy a house or start a business. They do this by using the money that people have deposited in the bank. When you borrow money from a bank, you have to pay it back with a little extra money, called interest, as well.

Banks also provide other services, like helping people to save for big purchases, like a car or college, and they also offer things like checking accounts and debit cards to make it easier to pay for things.

Overall, banks play an important role in helping people manage their money and achieve their financial goals.

Banks are important because they provide a safe place for people to keep their money, help people borrow money when they need it, and offer various financial services for people to manage their money.

If banks did not exist, it would be much harder for people to save money, borrow money and make payments.

It would also be challenging for businesses to access the funds they need to grow and create jobs. Overall, the economy would not function as smoothly without the important role that banks play.

‘

‘**Knowledge** is not free.
You have to **pay attention**.’

RICHARD FEYNMAN

Chapter 12

The Financial Statements

Once your business is set up, funds have been raised and operations have commenced, you will need to keep track of the incomes and expenses and to ensure that the business is headed in the right direction.

You will need to know whether the business is making a profit or a loss. You will want to know where the money that you have earned has gone.

For this you will have to maintain accounts and prepare periodic financial statements like the Profit and Loss Statement and the Balance Sheet.

The accounts should be maintained and these statements should be prepared by qualified and trained accountants. Unless you are one yourself, don't try making these on your own and leave the job to professionals.

But you as the business owner must know and understand what these statements reveal, and therefore a working knowledge of what goes into the making of these statements will be of help.

What are accounts?

Accounts are a record of all financial transactions that take place in an organization during a particular period.
Each time a financial transaction takes place, there is someone called an accountant whose job is to meticulously track such transactions and record them.
A collection of such records is called accounts.

Why do organizations maintain accounts?

As you know, the primary reason to start any business enterprise is to make profit.

If accounts are not maintained, you will not know in which direction the business is heading, whether it is making profit or loss, whether one should continue running it or shut it down.

How do you prepare the financial statements?

All transactions that take place get recorded, and whatever gets recorded periodically gets compressed and presented in the form of two financial statements—a Profit & Loss Statement and a Balance Sheet.

A Profit & Loss Statement is a statement that reveals whether a business has made a profit or a loss.

A business is said to have made profit when the **income** earned by it is greater than the **expenses** incurred. If it is vice versa, it has made a loss. To make a P&L statement, you need to list all the money you earned and all the money you spent during a specific time period, like a month or a year.

First, you add up the money you earned from things like selling products or providing services. Then, you subtract the money you spent on things like supplies, rent and salaries. The result is your profit or loss for that time period.

A Balance Sheet, on the other hand, lists out the **Liabilities** and **Assets** of an organization.

The liabilities reveal what you owe (or where the money raised by the business has come from—you owe it because you have borrowed it) and the assets represent where it was spent.

To make a Balance Sheet, you need to list all the things your business owns, like equipment and inventory, and all the things your business owes, like loans and bills. This helps you understand how much your business is worth and how well it is doing financially.

Now, this is important for you to understand, so I'm going to repeat it: All financial transactions get recorded as part of accounts. And when accounts are summarized, the result is presented in the form of a Profit & Loss Statement and a Balance Sheet.

This means that everything that happens in an organization over a certain period must eventually appear either on the face of the Profit & Loss Statement or the Balance Sheet.

The P&L Statement and the Balance Sheet together reveal just about four types of transactions: Expenses, Incomes, Assets and Liabilities.

This tells you that nothing can happen in an organization which is not eventually going to be categorized as one out of these four. There are only four possible classifications for any transaction that takes place in an organization.

So, if you wish to make these financial statements the non-accountant's way, all you have to do is look at every transaction that takes place, examine it, assess whether it is an expense, an income, an asset or a liability and record it accordingly. Your Profit & Loss Statement and Balance Sheet will now be ready.

Imagine for a moment that your organization takes a decision to stop maintaining accounts.

Instead, it keeps a large box in the middle of the entrance lobby.

Now each time a financial transaction takes place, instead of recording it in the books, someone writes it on a piece of paper and drops it into the box.

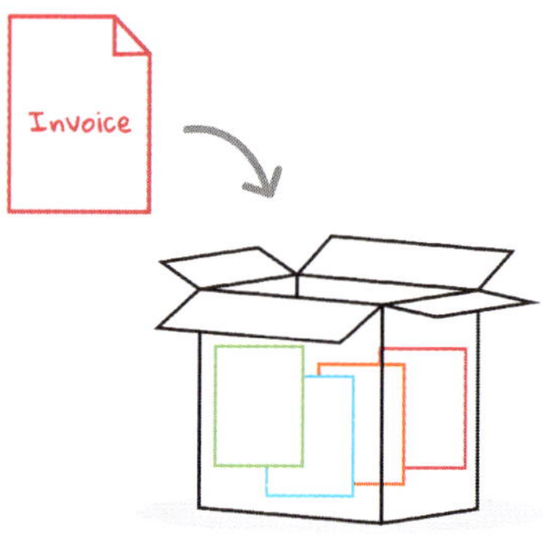

At the end of a certain period, this box is given to you and you are asked to make a Profit & Loss Statement and a Balance Sheet.

Can you do it?

Of course you can.

How will you go about it?

First of all, keep a template of a Profit & Loss and a Balance Sheet in front of you, as shown here.

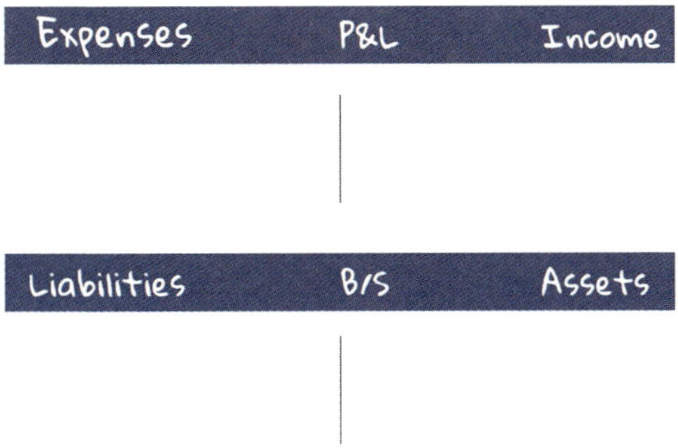

Now, put your hand in the box, take out the pieces of paper one at a time, look at the item listed and try to identify whether it is an income, an expense, an asset or a liability, and record it accordingly.

Let's say, on the first piece of paper, is written **salary**. Where will you record this? This appears to be an expense.

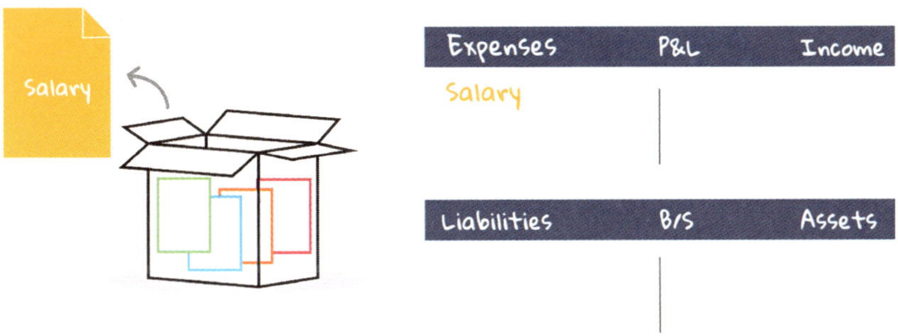

The next piece says 'travelling costs'. Also an expense.

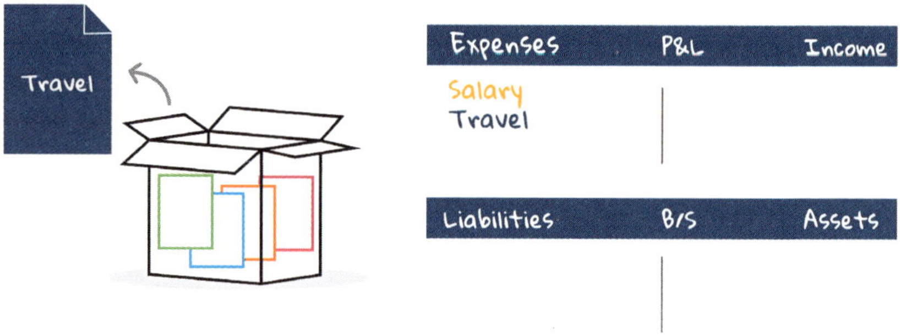

Goods or services sold? This is an income.

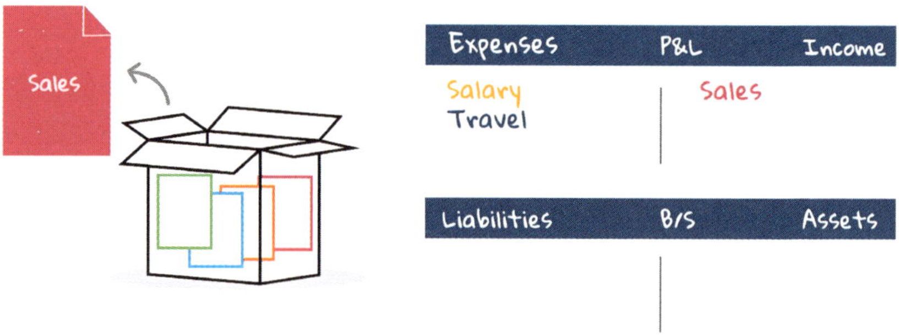

Loan taken? That's a liability.

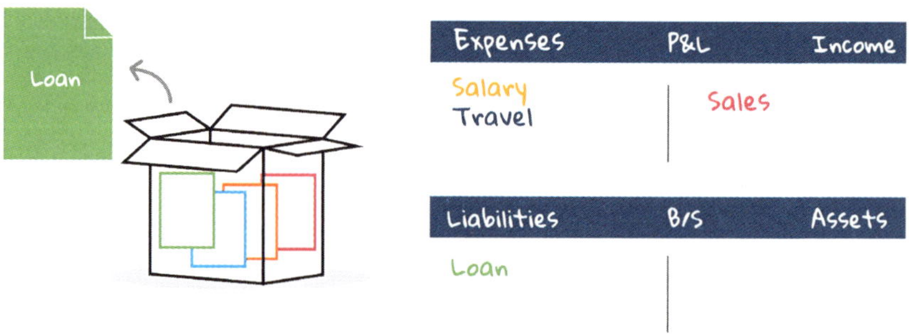

Car purchased? An asset.

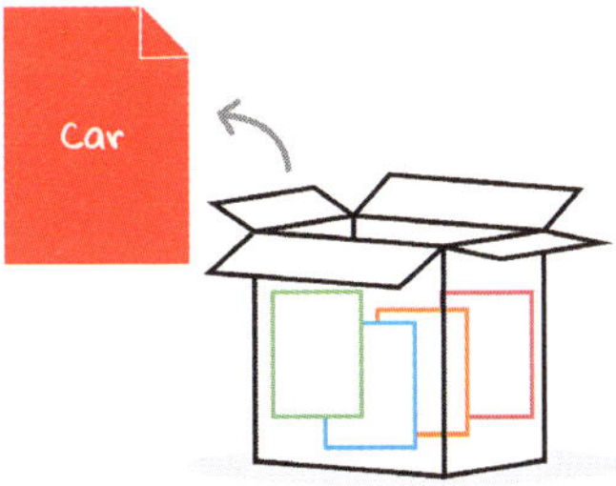

Expenses	P&L	Income
Salary Travel		Sales

Liabilities	B/S	Assets
Loan		Car

Interest paid on the loan? An expense, of course.

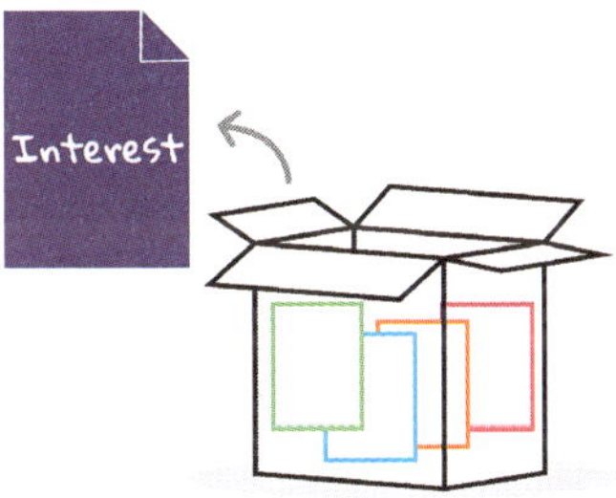

Expenses	P&L	Income
Salary Travel Interest		Sales

Liabilities	B/S	Assets
Loan		Car

Rent paid? This is an expense.

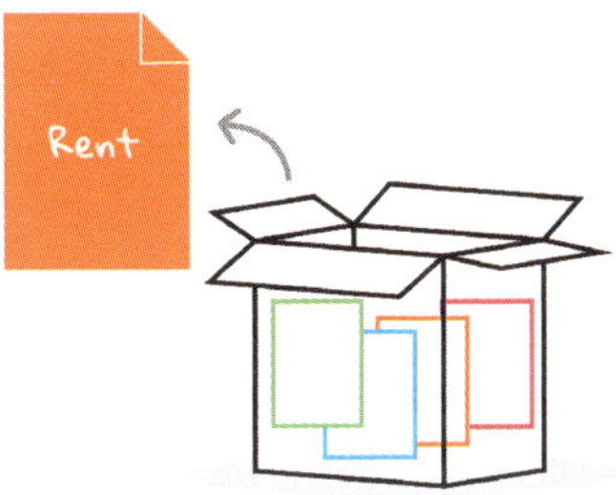

Expenses	P&L	Income
Salary Travel Interest Rent		Sales

Liabilities	B/S	Assets
Loan		Car

Money invested in stocks and shares of other companies? Assets.

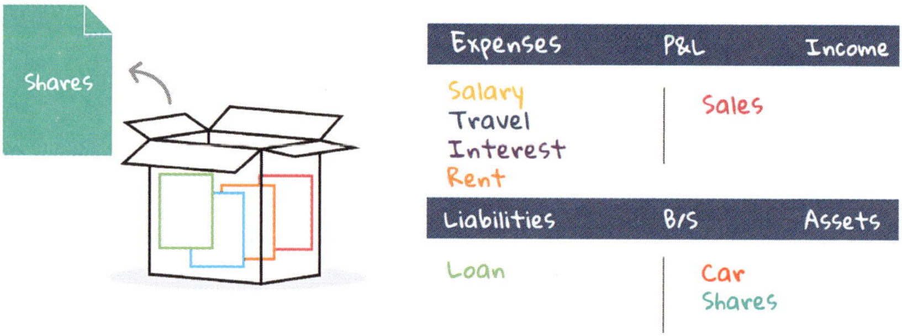

Dividends received on these stocks? Income.

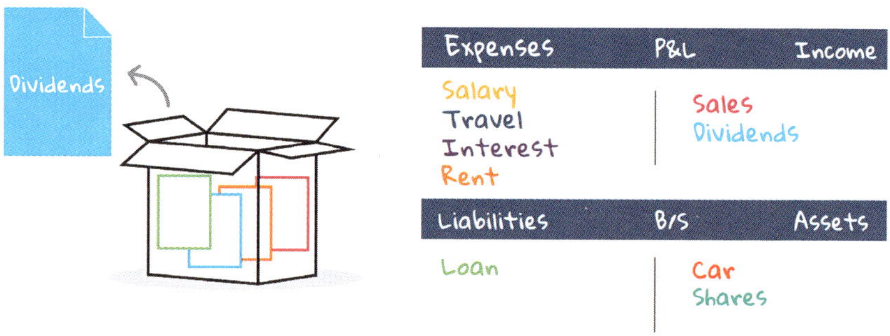

We can go on and on in this manner, and you will see that for every financial transaction you come up with (or every piece of paper that you take out of the box), you will be able to classify it as either an income, an expense, an asset or a liability.

At the end of the process, you will find that the Balance Sheet you have prepared using our layman's method is identical to the Balance Sheet prepared by your accountant.

‘

'Do not fear **failure**,
be **terrified** of regret.'

DESHAUNA BARBER

INCOME TAX— WHY DO WE PAY IT?

CHAPTER 13

Once you start earning money, you will have to pay income tax.

Now what is this, you may well ask.
And why do we have to pay it?

Let me try and answer these questions.

What is income tax?

As the name itself suggests, it is a tax on income.

What is a tax?

A tax is a statutory, mandatory payment made to the government.

And, therefore, what is income tax?

When the amount to be paid is a percentage of the income, it is called *Income Tax*.

When we pay to the government a percentage of the value of goods manufactured, it is called *Excise Duty*.

When it is a percentage of goods entering into the country, it is called *Customs Duty*.

When it is a percentage of the value of goods entering a city—*Octroi*.
When it is a percentage of the value of goods sold—*VAT*.

Percentage of the value of services rendered—*Service Tax*.

Most of these have now been replaced by the GST—the Goods and Services Tax—in India.

We keep paying the government in a variety of ways.
Yet another way in which we pay is when it is a percentage of our income. Then the tax is called income tax.

Should we pay income tax?

It doesn't matter how much it may hurt people to pay taxes, whenever I ask this question, invariably the answer is 'Of course, we should pay.'

What really hurts people is not so much the paying as the misuse of the money paid. If people were sure that the taxes paid will actually be used for the purpose for which they were collected, more people would pay happily.

Why do we pay taxes?

Taxes are obviously paid so that governments can raise the resources to pay for the various facilities provided for us, which none of us can provide for ourselves individually.

Even if I don't go into complicated theories of taxation and take some blatant examples of services and amenities that the government provides—roads, street lighting, police, the army—all of which are of a nature that it is neither possible nor affordable for citizens of a country to obtain on their own.

I mean, if the government asks all of us to build a road for, say, a hundred metres outside our respective homes, a majority of us will not be able to afford it.

But how many miles and miles of roads do we use?
We use postal services. We use the railways. The police is there to protect us. Without the army guarding our borders, we probably would be slaves to some marauding and ambitious rogue nation.

So, the logic of income tax (as other taxes) is that, all of us use the facilities and hence all of us must pay.

The problem of income tax is—all of us use the facilities, but all of us don't pay. Not only that all of us don't pay, but all of us can't pay.

And why can't all of us pay?

This is because a large percentage of our population lives below what is known as the Poverty Line.

What does it mean when we say that someone is living BPL (below the poverty line)?

Very often, a person living below the poverty line does not even earn enough to have three meals a day. By some estimates, almost 30 per cent of our population falls into this category.

I said earlier that the logic of collecting tax is that all of us enjoy the facilities, therefore all of us must pay.

Can this 30 per cent afford to pay? Are they even bothered whether the roads have potholes and whether the street lights are functioning effectively or not. They are struggling merely to survive.
That leaves us with the remaining 70 per cent, the ones that are above the line.

Now, so far as income tax is concerned, the government's stand is that it doesn't want you to pay income tax unless you lead a relatively decent life. The income tax act lays down that if a person earns less than a certain minimum amount every year, there is no need to pay any income tax.

Out of the 70 per cent that are APL (above the poverty line), perhaps 60 per cent earn less than the minimum required to pay income tax.

Now we are left with some 10 per cent of the population that is not only APL but has a surplus above the minimum amount that is tax-free out of which they can pay income tax.

And of this 10 per cent, about 70 per cent are tax evaders. *(These percentages are not exact but approximations and are merely intended to be illustrative.)*

Do you see how grave the situation is?

A while ago, I had posed a question: 'Should we pay taxes?' My answer is, of course we should. If for no other reason than as a token of thanksgiving that we happen to occupy the top 10 per cent slot of this nation's population, the least we can do is pay our taxes honestly.

The brighter side of taxation

Up to now, I have painted a very bleak picture of the tax situation illustrating how just a minuscule percentage of the population pays taxes.

Let me now show you the brighter side of the picture.

Let's take the case of income tax alone. I receive income and I pay tax on it.

What do I do with this money?

I have needs. Let's say I am a salaried person and I have been waiting to receive my salary so that I can purchase a shirt for myself. I receive my salary, pay income tax, and then go and spend this money on a shirt. This money goes from my pocket to the pocket of the shirt seller. It becomes the shirt seller's income. She pays tax on it.

Maybe, she has been wanting to buy a pair of shoes. When she spends this money, it becomes the shoe seller's income. The shoe seller pays tax on it.

Do you realize each time a rupee merely changes hands, it becomes somebody's income and the government gets a share of it?

It has been estimated that out of every rupee that is made, more than 97 paise goes back to the government by way of income tax alone.

Once I was thinking aloud, why only 97 paise? Why not 5 rupees? And someone pointed out, that is probably because, by the time 97 paise get collected, the rupee must be getting worn out and discarded.

And this is **income tax** alone. I earn a rupee, I pay income tax. If I use that money to purchase an asset, and if I still own that asset on 31 March, it becomes part of my wealth on which I must pay **wealth tax**.

And having paid income tax and wealth tax, a little later, in one of my generous moods, if I gift the item to somebody, I would have had to pay **gift tax**.

And a little later, if I happen to die, somebody on my behalf would have to pay **estate duty** on the wealth left behind by me.

Mercifully, in India, many years ago, estate duty was abolished. Subsequently, donor-based gift tax also got abolished. Wealth tax provisions were diluted to such an extent that a far smaller percentage than before are now liable to pay it. The formula to calculate long-term capital gains was tweaked to introduce the concept of cost inflation index that substantially reduced the tax on capital gains. The tax rates on long-term capital gains were also reduced. The highest marginal tax rate, which in the 1960s was a ridiculous 98 per cent, and even at the start of the liberalization process in 1991 was 60 and 55 per cent respectively for corporate and personal tax payers, was reduced to 30 per cent, and in some cases to 25 per cent.

Today, taxpayers in India really do not have any reason to complain.

‘

'The **hardest thing** in the world to understand is the **income tax**.'

ALBERT EINSTEIN

THE BIG LEAP

CHAPTER 14

You are now ready to take the leap

Let's say, a few years down the line, your business has become fairly big. You have gained significant experience, developed an impressive network of clients and vendors, and are brimming with confidence. You are now ready to take a big leap forward, and for this you need a large sum of money—let's say, rupees ten million, that is, one crore. (I was going to say a hundred or a thousand crores, but then there will be too many zeroes involved and it may become difficult to explain what I have in mind).

Where will this money come from?

Raising a large sum of money from 1 or 2 individuals can be difficult. But the same result can be achieved by taking small sums of money from a large number of individuals.

So you decide to take the latter route and make a public issue of shares (an Initial Public Offering or an IPO). This is also known as raising funds through the primary market.

You aim to collect 100 rupees each from 100,000 people.

But the question is, why would these people agree to give you this money? What are you offering them in return?

So you tell them that you will make them partners in your business. These partners, or co-owners, will now be called **shareholders**.

If you have taken a hundred rupees each from 100,000 individuals, you will now have a hundred thousand shareholders in your business.

Who will run the business?

Before the IPO, you were the sole owner, taking all the decisions. Now there are a hundred thousand owners. How will the business now be run? Who will take the decisions? There can be complete chaos.

The answer to this question is provided in the Companies Act, which contains the law that governs the running of all private and public limited companies.

The law, amongst other things, says that whenever there are multiple owners (in this case, the shareholders), the owners will elect representatives from amongst themselves who will run the company on their behalf.

This is similar to a situation that exists in any democratic country.

In a democracy, there are no rulers or kings. The country belongs to all of us. But all of us can't go and sit in parliament, else pandemonium will ensue.

So who will run the country on our behalf?

The law provides that all citizens must elect candidates who will represent them in parliament. The party that wins the majority seats will elect a leader called the Prime Minister. And this is how the country will be governed.

Similarly, in the case of a company, the shareholders elect what is known as the Board of Directors, who will choose, from amongst themselves, a Managing Director, and the board led by the MD are empowered to take most of the decisions to govern and run the company.

What are you worried about?

You are the one who started this business. Due to your initial success and the experience gained by you, you had the confidence to scale up the business exponentially. For this, you needed a large sum of money, for which you approached many individuals. To convince them to invest with you, you promised to make them co-owners.

A legitimate concern of yours will be, now that there are 100,000 owners besides you, how will you continue retaining control over the company.

If these co-owners do not elect you to the board, you could land up losing control of the business that you had started.

This could very well happen, unless you take some precautions.

You—the original founder—must ensure that you are elected not only to the board of directors but also remain the managing director?

How will you do that?

One method is, you should hold the majority shares yourself.

How will that help?

To understand this, let us consider the similarities and the difference between a country's and a company's elections.

Similarities:

In a country, all citizens vote.
In a company, all shareholders vote.

In a country, all citizens are equal.
In a company, all shareholders are equal.
(These are equity shareholders, which also implies equality. If one person became a shareholder 20 years ago and another bought the shares 20 minutes back, the company cannot give more dividends

(or any other benefit) to the former. Both will be considered as equals.)

In a country, each citizen has one vote.
And herein lies the difference—in a company, each shareholder does not have one vote. Each share has one vote.

If you have one share and I have two, I'm twice as equal as you are. If you hold majority shares in your company, you will also command majority votes.

So if you hold majority shares, all you have to do is to stand for elections and vote for yourself. You don't care if the others vote for you or not.

Not practically workable

However, this may not be a practical solution, since to have 51 per cent shares, you will need to invest 51 per cent of the money.

The reason why you made the public issue of shares in the first place was you didn't have the money and wanted to raise most of it from outsiders.

Anybody can keep control over a company with a majority share holding. But is it possible to invest a miniscule percentage of your own money and take the bulk of it from strangers, and still retain control over the company?
(As Mark Twain said, 'If man bites dog, that is news.')

There are many cases where the promoters have held less than 10 per cent, in some cases less than 5 per cent and in a few cases even just about one-half per cent of the shares and still remained in control of the businesses.

For this, you have to resort to smarter methods else you may land up losing the company to a predator who buys more shares than you from the open market.

You must look up the case of Lord Swraj Paul, who attempted to takeover Escorts Ltd and Delhi Cloth and General Mills Ltd (DCM) in 1983. The promoters of Escorts (the Nanda family headed by Mr H.P. Nanda) held around 6 per cent of the company's shares and Mr Bharatram (DCM) held approximately 9 per cent of the company's shares, making them vulnerable to a hostile takeover.

Since their holdings were small, Swraj Paul attempted to gain control by purchasing shares from the open market and from financial institutions. However, he failed in the attempt.

'Better than **1000 days** of diligent study by oneself is one day with a **great mentor**.'

ANCIENT JAPANESE PROVERB

PART

D

LET'S TAKE A MACRO VIEW

CHAPTER 15

FINANCE MANAGEMENT OF NATIONS

Where does the government get money from to run the nation?

What is the budget that the government presents each year?

Do the principles of good finance management that apply to a business also apply to the managing of a country?

What is inflation and what causes it?

If these questions have ever come to your mind and you were looking for answers, then read on.

Where does the government get money from to run the nation?

A government's receipts can broadly be broken up into two parts:
1) Earnings and
2) Borrowings

Its earnings come from taxes levied on individuals and businesses which can be further broken up into **a) direct taxes** and **b) indirect taxes**.

Governments also borrow. These are from internal as well as external sources.

Each time you and I invest money in government bonds or deposit schemes like the PPF (Public Provident Fund), it is a loan given to the government, which it has to return after a fixed duration.

External sources include loans that governments take from other countries and the World Bank or the IMF (International Monetary Fund), etc.

What is the budget that the government presents each year?

Every year, the finance minister presents a budget to the nation.

A budget contains an estimate of the receipts and the expenditures for the year ahead.

The receipts are broken up into **revenue receipts** (money that the government earns) and **capital receipts** (the money that it borrows).

Similarly, the expenditures are divided into **revenue expenditures** (money that the government will spend on administrative purposes like salaries to be paid to government employees, money to be spent on guarding the nation internally and externally, interest on loans taken, etc.) and **capital expenditures** (money to be spent on creating infrastructure in the country—roads, airports, bridges, dams, etc.)

Budget

Expenditures	Receipts
Revenue Expenditure (Administrative expenses, salaries, interest, etc.)	**Revenue Receipts** (Earnings)
Capital Expenditure (Administrative expenses, salaries, interest, etc.)	**Capital Receipts** (Borrowings)

A budget is a projection of what is expected to happen in the coming one year, and the receipts and expenditures are just estimates, a statement of intention, so to say.

When this estimate is prepared, sometimes it may happen that the expected receipts may be greater than the expected expenditures (in which case it is called a **surplus budget**), or the expected expenditures may be greater than the expected receipts (in which case it is called a **deficit budget**).

In an extremely rare case, it may happen that the receipts and expenditure match. It will then be called a **balanced budget**.

If the receipts exceed the expenditures, there is no problem, but what happens when the budget is a deficit one? Which would mean that the government plans to spend more that what it will earn and borrow? Where will it get the money from to meet the deficit?

In such cases, the only option available to the government is to print (or create) more money.

When money gets printed in order to meet the deficit, it is called deficit financing.

And the fallout of this tendency on the part of the government to print money and spend is **inflation**.

Let's understand the causes of inflation and its repercussions?

What is inflation?

Inflation refers to a phenomenon of either rising prices or falling purchasing powers. And I just mentioned that inflation is caused by deficit financing resorted to by the government.

What's the connection?

Why does deficit financing lead to inflation?

I mean, the government needed to spend, so it printed money. Why did it result in an increase in the price of the bread at the bakery?

To understand this, we must understand how prices of goods and services are determined.

Prices, as you already know, are a result of the function of **demand** and **supply**.

Consider an example:

If one group of people—let's call them Group A—is engaged in the manufacture of cars and another group—Group B—is in need of cars.

The capacity of Group A is to make 100 cars and the requirement of Group B is for 100 cars.

If a car sells for 100,000, chances are it will continue to sell at that price.

Now imagine one person gets added to Group B and their requirement of cars goes up to 101. The capacity of Group A to manufacture cars is still 100.

What do you think will happen to the price of cars?

It will go up.

When the demand for a product or commodity goes up, its price goes up.

What if one person gets added to Group A, and they now make 101 cars. But the requirement of cars of Group B is still 100.

What will happen to the price?

It will fall.

When the supply of a product or commodity goes up, its price comes down.

Each time demand goes up, will price go up?
Each time that supply increases, will price fall?

Not necessarily.

In the above case, when Group B's requirement for cars went up to 101, what if Group A had responded by making 101 cars? The price would not have gone up.

So, the maxim gets modified slightly:
When the demand for a product or commodity goes up, its price goes up, unless supply responds.

When Group A manufactures 101 cars and Group B is willing to purchase 101 cars, the price will not fall.

When the supply for a product or commodity goes up, its price will fall, unless demand responds.

In order for price to rise or fall, it is necessary that there is unilateral increase either in demand or supply.

Why is deficit financing inflationary?

For a moment, imagine each person in the country earns 'x' amount of money per month.

In the following year, everybody works twice as hard and starts earning '2x' per month.

The spending power of the entire population has gone up.

The buying power of the nation has doubled.

Will it lead to price rise?

The answer is, no!

Why not?

How did the buying power double?

It is because everyone worked twice as hard.

Which means they must have also produced twice as much.

While, on the one hand, the buying power has doubled, on the other hand, the supply of goods and services has also doubled.

It is non-inflationary.

But when governments print money to spend, there is merely an increase in the supply of money without a corresponding increase in the supply of goods and services. More money now chases the same quantity of goods and services, and this leads to inflation.

If there is inflation, so what?

Is inflation good or bad for an economy?

Asking this question is as ridiculous as asking, 'Is having blood pressure good or bad for a body?'

Should a human body have blood pressure?

Of course, it should. No blood pressure is a sign of a dead body.

Similarly, no inflation is a sign of a dead economy. Alive and kicking economies are bound to have inflation.

Just as in the case of blood pressure, the problem does not lie with inflation. It becomes a problem when it is either more or even when it is low.

One of the key responsibilities of a government is to manage the twin goals of achieving a healthy growth rate and at the same time not letting inflation get out of hand.

Quite an unenvious task, you will appreciate. There are some countries in the world striving to create inflation while others are busy fighting to bring it under control.

How can inflation be tamed?

This question is easy to answer in theory.

What causes inflation in the first place?
The pumping of money into the economy.

So what will bring it down?
Sucking the money out of the economy.

Easier said than done.

How do you go about doing it?

Inflation occurs when demand exceeds supply. To control inflation, either demand must come down or supply must go up.

In democracies, governments don't control the supply, which is predominantly in private hands.

What the government can control, however, is the demand.

To reduce demand, it is essential that money in the pockets of the citizens should reduce.

For this, governments have two weapons in their arsenal—**the fiscal policy** and **the monetary policy**—the former dealing with the tax rates and the latter controlling the interest rates.

If the government wishes to reduce the money available to spend with the citizens in order to curb demand, then a fiscal policy measure would be to raise taxes.

However, the reason governments gets frantic when inflation rates are high is the fear of losing votes. The voting public perceives unbridled inflation as a failure of the government and a black mark against its functioning. Many a government has lost power due to its inability to rein in inflation.

If the primary driving force to tame inflation was the desire to stay in power and garner more votes, raising taxes to bring inflation down would be a self-defeating move since, while it will no doubt serve the purpose of reducing inflation, it will by no means enhance the government's image in the eyes of the electorate.

Most popularity-conscious, voter-pleasing governments would shun this measure.

The only other measure available to the government is the use of the monetary policy.

The central bank will then announce a hike in the interest rates.

What happens when interest rates go up?

Those who deposit money in banks stand to earn more and those who borrow from banks pay more.

Depositing money becomes more attractive and borrowing less.

More people deposit money, less people borrow, resulting in

money moving from the pockets of the people into the coffers of the banks.

The central bank, using tools like the cash reserve and the liquidity ratios, withdraws the money out of circulation.

When money supply in the economy comes down, inflation also comes down.

What role does interest play in an economy?

The role of interest in an economy is to beat inflation.

Have you heard of a term called **real rate of interest**?

Whenever you read the word 'real', it should be taken to mean 'net of inflation'.

If the nominal rate of interest offered by the bank is 6 per cent and the rate of inflation is 4 per cent, it would mean that the real rate of interest is 2 per cent.

The real rate of interest in an economy, as far as possible, should not be negative. This would be the case if the bank offers, say, 6 per cent and the inflation is at 9 per cent.

In such cases, the depositor starts feeling like a fool and starts regretting saving the money, feeling she would have been better off had she spent it instead.

If the real rate of interest remains negative over a long period, it can have serious implications.

If one had visited Mexico in the early 1980s, one would have seen huge billboards in various places displaying advertisements by banks inviting deposits and offering interest rates as high as 80 per cent.

Sounds too high?

Not if you consider that at that time, the rate of inflation in Mexico was in excess of 100 per cent.

Prior to 1991 (when India started the liberalization process), India had an average inflation rate of 9 per cent. At that time, the banks then were paying 10 per cent on deposits and the loans were available at around 12 per cent.

Germany at one time had a 6–6.5 per cent inflation. Banks were paying around 7 per cent and one could borrow at 7.5 to 8 per cent.

Japan, some years back, had negative inflation. Those days banks were levying a service charge on money lying in the bank.

The underlying logic is very simple. When there is inflation, that is, demand is in excess of supply, you have to discourage spending. So interest rates need to be higher in order to encourage people to save.

During recessions, the reverse is happening—demand lags behind supply. Now people need to be dissuaded from saving and encouraged to spend in order to generate demand. So they are penalized for saving.

Is there a good deficit?

As already discussed, when the expected receipts in a budget are lesser than the expected expenditures, it results in a deficit.

Is a budgetary deficit always bad, or can there be a good deficit too?

Say that the total budgeted receipts are 100 and the expenditure 120, resulting in a budgetary deficit of 20. How will this deficit be met?

By printing of notes.

Examine three scenarios that can result in a deficit.

Let's say, in all the three scenarios, the receipts are equally divided between revenue and capital, that is, earnings are 50 and borrowings are also 50.

Is there a good deficit?

Budget

Expenditures

	C	B	A
Revenue Exp	40	80	60
Revenue Deficit/Surplus	10	30	10
Capital Exp	80	40	60
Capital Deficit/Surplus	30	10	10
	120	120	120
Budgetary Deficit	20	20	20

Receipts

Revenue Receipts (Earnings)	50
Capital Receipts (Borrowings)	50
	100

On the expenditure side:

1. In scenario A, the revenue expenditure is 60 and the capital expenditure is also 60. There is a revenue deficit of 10 and also a deficit on the capital account of 10, leading to a budgetary deficit of 20.

2. In scenario B, the revenue expenditure is 80 and the capital expenditure is 40. Which means, there is a revenue deficit of 30 and a capital surplus of 10, and thus a budgetary deficit of 20.

3. In scenario C, the revenue expenditure is 40 and the capital expenditure is 80. That is, there is a revenue surplus of 10 and a capital deficit of 30, resulting in a budgetary deficit of 20.

Which scenario is desirable? Which is the best deficit to have?

In scenario A, there is a deficit on both the counts. Neither are the expected revenue receipts sufficient to cover revenue expenditures, nor the capital receipts to cover capital expenditure.

However, in scenario B, the revenue receipts fall short of the revenue expenditure by 30. But the expected capital receipts are more than the expenditure, resulting in a surplus of 10. This surplus must have been used to contribute towards the revenue deficit of 30, and the balance deficit would be met by the creation or printing of money.

So, in this case, it looks like the government plans to borrow money and use it for revenue expenditure, such as payment of salaries and interest on loans, etc. And they also plan to print money and use it for the same purpose.

Will you borrow money to purchase a house? Maybe. Will you borrow money to pay rent? I hope not. You should be able to meet the expenditure on rent from your earnings.

In scenario C, the expected revenue receipts are 50 and the planned revenue expenditures are 40, resulting in a revenue surplus of 10.

As far as the capital receipts and expenditures are concerned, there is a deficit of 30.

This indicates that the expenditure of 80 on capital account, that is, for developmental purposes and the building of infrastructure, will be met to the extent of 10 from the surplus on revenue account, another 50 will come from internal and external borrowings, and the balance 20 will be met through printing of money.

By all means, print notes and give the country better roads and infrastructure. But don't print money to meet the expenditure on account of inefficient underutilized- over-employed government staff.

Do the rules of good finance management that apply to a business also apply to the running of a nation?

Coming back to the question I had asked you in the beginning of this chapter, do the rules of good finance management that apply to corporations also apply to a nation?

In my earlier book *Romancing The Balance Sheet,* I had prescribed two rules which, if followed, ensure sustained growth and prosperity, and if violated, extract a price and could even lead to the failure of a business.

The second of these rules was that a healthy organization must ensure that it uses long-term funds for long-term purposes and short-term funds for short-term purposes.

There is no harm if long-term funds are used for short-term purposes. But it should *never* use short-term funds for long-term purposes.

In a similar vein, nations must ensure that revenue expenditures are met out of revenue receipts.

Capital receipts should be used for capital expenditure.

While it is fine to use revenue surplus to meet capital expenditure, a situation to be avoided at all costs is using capital surplus to meet revenue deficits.

'It is not because of the **benevolence of the baker** that we eat fresh bread every morning but because of his **desire to make money**.'

UNKNOWN

TERMS USED

01. **Angel investors:** Angel investors are individuals who provide financial backing for small start-ups or entrepreneurs.

02. **Asset:** An asset is something of value that is owned by an individual or company.

03. **Average rate of return:** The average rate of return is a measure of the profitability of an investment over a specified period of time.

04. **Balance sheet:** A balance sheet is a financial statement that shows a company's assets, liabilities and shareholders' equity at a specific point in time.

05. **Bonds:** Bonds are a type of debt investment where an investor loans money to an entity for a defined period of time at a fixed interest rate.

06. **Bootstrapping:** Bootstrapping is a method of starting a business with minimal external funding or resources.

07. **Branding:** Branding is the process of creating and promoting a unique image and identity for a company's products or services.

08. **Break-even point:** The break-even point is the level of sales at which a company's total revenue equals its total expenses, resulting in neither profit nor loss.

09. **Business plan:** A business plan is a document that outlines a company's goals, strategies and projected financial performance. It's like a roadmap for the business.

10. **Cash flow:** Cash flow is the movement of money into or out of a business, typically measured over a specific period of time.

11. **Cash flow statement:** A cash flow statement is a financial report that shows the amount of money coming into and going out of a company over a specific period of time.

12. **Compound interest:** Compound interest is a method of calculating interest on a loan or investment where the interest is calculated on the initial principal and also on the accumulated interest from previous periods.

13. **Convertible debt:** Convertible debt is a type of loan that can be converted into equity in the company at a later date.

14. **Creditor:** A creditor is a person or entity to whom money is owed by a debtor.

15. **Customer segmentation:** Customer segmentation is the process of dividing a company's customer base into groups based on similar characteristics, such as age, gender or buying behaviour.

16. **Debentures:** Debentures are a type of debt instrument that is issued by a company and which usually provides a fixed rate of interest.

17. **Debt:** Debt is money that is borrowed and must be repaid, usually with interest.

18. **Debtor:** A debtor is a person or entity that owes money to another person or entity.

19. **Direct tax:** A direct tax is a tax that is imposed directly on an individual or entity, such as income tax.

20. **Discounted cash flow:** Discounted cash flow is a method used to value an investment by discounting its expected future cash flows to their present value.

21. **Entrepreneur:** An entrepreneur is a person who starts and runs a business, taking on financial risks in the hope of making a profit.

22. **Equity:** Equity is the ownership interest in a company. If you own equity in a company, you own a piece of that company.

23. **Equity Shares:** Equity shares are units of ownership in a company. If you own equity shares, you are a part owner of the company.

24. **Expense:** An expense is the cost of goods or services used to generate revenue.

25. **Fixed deposit:** A fixed deposit is a type of investment where money is deposited in a bank or financial institution for a fixed period of time at a fixed interest rate.

26. **Founder:** A founder is a person who establishes a company or organization.

27. **Income:** Income is the money earned from various sources, such as wages, salaries and investments.

28. **Income statement:** An income statement is a financial report that shows a company's revenue, expenses and profit or loss over a specific period of time, such as a month or a year.

29. **Indirect tax:** An indirect tax is a tax that is imposed on goods and services, such as sales tax or value-added tax.

30. **Internal rate of return:** The internal rate of return is a metric used to estimate the profitability of an investment.

31. **Liability:** A liability is a financial obligation or debt owed by an individual or company.

32. **Loss:** Loss is the opposite of profit. It occurs when a company's expenses are greater than its revenue, resulting in a negative amount of money.

33. **Market research:** Market research is the process of gathering and analysing information about a target market, including its size, demographics and preferences.

34. **Market share:** Market share is the percentage of total sales in a specific market that a company captures.

35. **Marketing strategy:** A marketing strategy is a plan for promoting and selling a company's products or services, including advertising, pricing and distribution.

36. **Pay back period:** The pay back period is the amount of time it takes for an investment to generate enough cash flow to cover the initial cost of the investment.

37. **Pitch deck:** A pitch deck is a presentation that entrepreneurs use to pitch their business ideas to potential investors.

38. **Preference shares:** Preference shares are a type of stock that gives shareholders certain rights, such as priority in receiving dividends.

39. **Present value of money:** The present value of money is the current value of a future sum of money, taking into account a specified rate of return.

40. **Profit:** Profit is the amount of money that a company earns after subtracting all its expenses from its total revenue. It's the money left over after paying all the bills.

41. **Promoter:** A promoter is a person or company that helps to organize and finance a business venture.

42. **Return on investment:** Return on investment (ROI) is a measure of the profitability of an investment, calculated as the ratio of the net profit to the initial cost of the investment.

43. **Revenue:** Revenue is the total amount of money that a company earns from its business activities, such as selling products or providing services.

44. **Risk management:** Risk management is the process of identifying, assessing and mitigating potential risks that could impact a company's operations or financial performance.

45. **Securities:** Securities are financial instruments that can be traded, and can represent ownership in a company or a claim on assets.

46. **Seed fund:** Seed fund is the initial capital used to start a business.

47. **Shareholders' agreement:** A shareholders' agreement is a contract between the shareholders of a company that outlines their rights and obligations.

48. **Supply and demand:** Supply and demand is the relationship between the availability of a product or service and the desire for it, which determines its price and quantity sold in the market.

49. **SWOT analysis:** SWOT analysis is a strategic planning tool that helps a company identify its strengths, weaknesses, opportunities and threats.

50. **Venture capitalist:** A venture capitalist is someone who invests money in new or growing companies in exchange for a share of the company's ownership. They take a risk in the hope of making a profit if the company does well.

SUNDAY MUSINGS ON FINANCE MANAGEMENT WITH ANIL LAMBA

SUNDAY MUSINGS

Every Sunday morning, I send out a short note on some aspect of finance management to a select group of people. These are usually powerful messages contained in a few words on which one can ruminate over the rest of the day.

If you too wish to receive these messages, you can scan the QR code given below and join the WhatsApp group.

Sunday Musings

ON FINANCE MANAGEMENT

Dr Anil Lamba

If, for any reason, you are unable to join the group, please go to **https://anillamba.com/sunday-musings/** and use the QR code given there.

OTHER TITLES BY DR ANIL LAMBA

Anil Lamba on Finance

A series of books on Finance Management

REVISED
+
UPDATED
EDITION
DRAWBRIDGE™
Romancing the
Balance
Sheet
For anyone who owns, runs
or manages a business
Anil Lamba

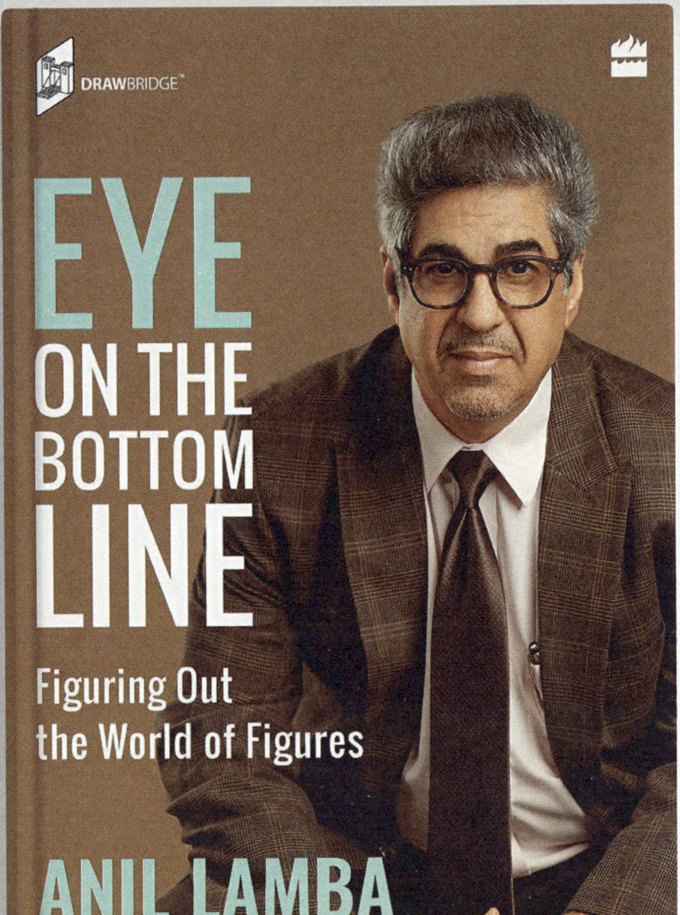
DRAWBRIDGE™
EYE ON THE BOTTOM LINE
Figuring Out the World of Figures
ANIL LAMBA
Author of the Bestseller
Romancing the Balance Sheet

DRAWBRIDGE™
'Monogamy is not a virtue in the stock market. "Flirt with many and marry a few" is the mantra here!'
Flirting with Stocks
Stock Market Investing for Beginners
ANIL LAMBA
BESTSELLING AUTHOR OF
ROMANCING THE BALANCE SHEET

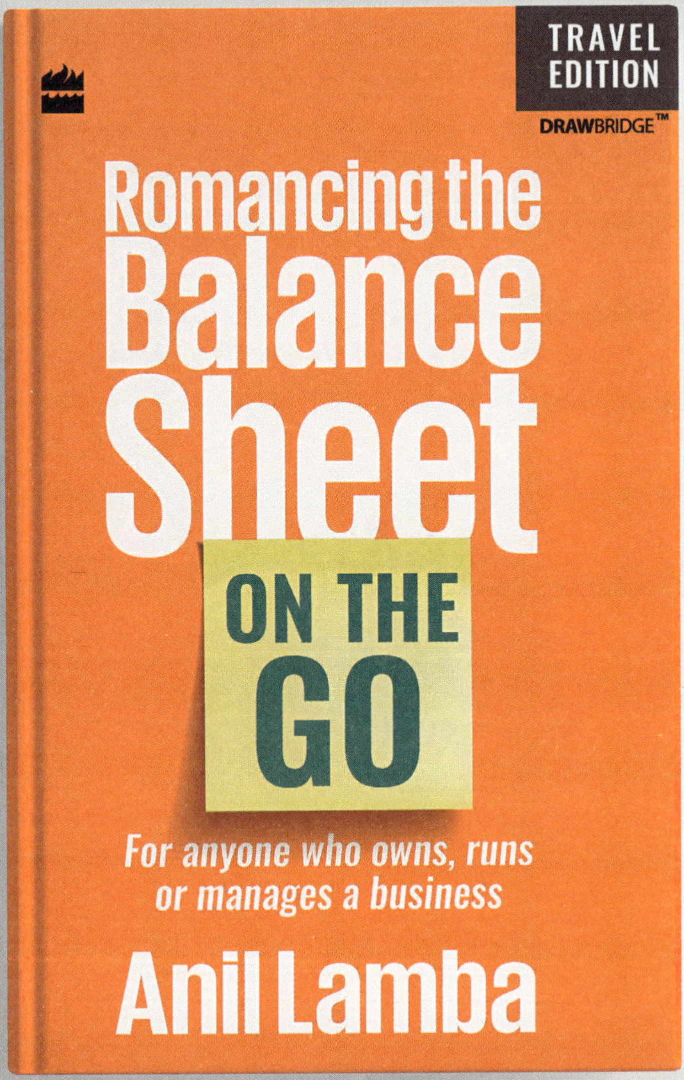
TRAVEL EDITION
DRAWBRIDGE™
Romancing the Balance Sheet
ON THE GO
For anyone who owns, runs or manages a business
Anil Lamba

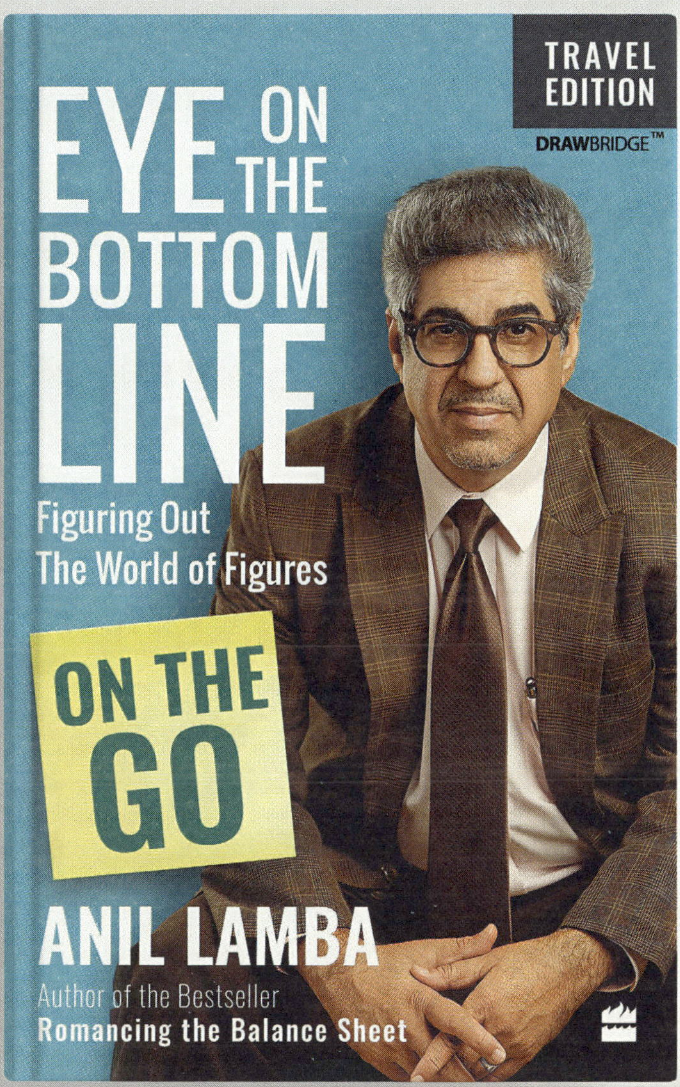
TRAVEL EDITION
DRAWBRIDGE™
EYE ON THE BOTTOM LINE
Figuring Out The World of Figures
ON THE GO
ANIL LAMBA
Author of the Bestseller
Romancing the Balance Sheet

FINANCIAL AFFAIRS OF THE COMMON MAN
Master The Art Of Personal Finance Management
ANIL LAMBA
Bestselling Author Of Romancing The Balance Sheet

Bestselling author of
Romancing the Balance Sheet
DRAW
BRIDGE
ANIL
LAMBA
Timeless
Wisdom
on Finance

About the Author

Dr Anil Lamba is a bestselling author, financial literacy activist and international corporate trainer. A chartered accountant with degrees in commerce and law as well as a doctorate in taxation, his training programmes are held internationally. Dr Lamba's client list exceeds three thousand large- and medium-sized corporations spread across India, the US, Europe, Russia, Africa, West Asia and the Far East.